God,
Are You Really There?

Mary Hornback

PublishAmerica
Baltimore

First printing

ISBN: 1-59286-659-X
PUBLISHED BY PUBLISHAMERICA BOOK
PUBLISHERS
www.publishamerica.com
Baltimore

Printed in the United States of America

DEDICATED TO:

My parents,
Albert & Phyliss Roth,
who brought me
to Jesus at an early age
and have given me their love,
prayers, and support.

Our very special grandchildren,
Maria, Christina, Mary, Christopher,
Tristan and Brooklyn
who have so much potential
and so much to give.

"And he took the children in His arms,
put His hands on them
and blessed them." Mark 10:16

Acknowledgements

Saying thank you does not begin to express my gratitude to all of those people who have made this book possible. My very special thanks to:

My husband Shelton (Shelly) and our children Kevin, Sheryl, and Greg—for your loving support and prayers and for allowing me to share from your lives.

My granddaughter Maria—for allowing me to use your picture on the cover of this book.

Jeannine Becker—for your encouragement and prayers and the ride to my parents' home every day to get me started.

Paul Meeks—for your encouragement that kept me going when I was ready to give up.

Rosemary Fenton—for the hours of time spent in proofreading. I couldn't have done it without you!

Beth Luebe—for proofreading and giving me some helpful suggestions.

Shirley Heller—for your good input.

Sue Willett—for pointing me to PublishAmerica.

Each of you who has willingly allowed me to share your stories. Your lives have been a great blessing to me as I pray they will be to many others.

Chapter 1

God, Are You There?

It seemed the past week had been filled with nothing but frustrations. I had finally decided to write God a letter and tell Him what was going on in my life (just in case He didn't know).

"Dear God," I wrote, "this week started by our son Greg's falling down the stairs. If he would have been coming down the steps at his usual fast pace with the back of him hardly keeping up with the front, I wouldn't have been surprised if he had fallen, but he wasn't feeling well that day and was dragging his feet. As a result, he tripped. He told me his wrist hurt, but not seeing anything abnormal, I smiled and told him he would soon feel better. When I waited most of the day, and he still didn't feel better, I finally decided to take him to the doctor. You can imagine how badly I felt when he ended up with a cast on his wrist. I had felt sure the doctor would say to go home and take aspirin.

"The next day our daughter Sheryl was riding her bike and got hit by a car. After what had happened the day before, I didn't waste any time getting her to the doctor. The black and blue marks told me she was hurting. This had to be serious! The policeman met us at the doctor's office, walking in with his blue uniform and clipboard and asking us a lot of questions. What did the doctor tell Sheryl to do? You guessed it. 'Go home and take aspirin!'

"The following day Greg somehow managed to get his wrist removed from his cast, so we were once again back to the doctor's office. I thought for sure they would name one of their rooms after us, but they didn't.

"Then there was the day I had to go shopping. It was very late, so I hurried as fast as I could to find my items and get into the checkout line. It was a long line, but it was finally my turn, and I gratefully put my things on the counter. The clerk rang them up, and then, to my consternation, I realized there weren't any blank checks in my check book! I asked the clerk if she would hold my items while I ran home. She said she would. When I returned a half hour later, my items had all been put back on the shelves! There was nothing I could do but scurry through the store and pick everything up again. With a sigh of relief, I finally checked out and went on my way. Turning on my car radio, I tried to relax. By the time I got home I was in a fairly good mood, that is until I discovered that I had brought only one of the two bags home from the store. I couldn't believe it! It was back to the store to get the other bag.

"That brings us to today. This afternoon I tried to iron and found my steam iron wasn't working properly. I finally realized the water I was pouring into the opening at the top was coming out the bottom. I remembered I had set the iron on the dryer a few days ago to cool. When I had turned on the dryer, the iron had jiggled off onto the floor. At least it still heats. (I do remember that before steam ironing days there used to be a thing called sprinkling.)

"So you see, God, this has not been a good week. I would really appreciate it if you would make sure things do not continue this way."

Of course, this is silly. We don't really talk to God this way, or do we? Sometimes when we have continual frustrations and pressures in our lives, we may at least feel like it. But what do we do about the real trials, the tragedies that come into our lives? How do we handle them? How do we keep going?

We don't have to look very far to find hurting, struggling people in this world. They are all around us. I cannot pretend to know the depth of grief many people face. As I picked up the newspaper this morning, I read, "DRIFTER KILLS FIVE STUDENTS." The article stated that all of these children were from refugee families from Southeast Asia. Many had known the horrors of war in their own homelands and had come here to start a new life. My question along with many others would have to be, "Why? Why did such a thing have to happen?" Headlines from other newspapers read, "STORY OF MISSOURI SLAYING: A TWISTED TALE WRAPPED IN SATANISM," "WOMAN DESCRIBES ATTACK IN RAPE CASE," "TESTIMONY OF KIDNAPPING VICTIM HEARD," "10-YEAR OLD SUSPECTED IN SHOOTING OF BUS DRIVER," and the list goes on and on.

There is nothing that can make up for the loss and heartache felt when these kinds of tragedies happen. They are revolting and cruel! It is at these times we may ask, "Where is God? Does He see me? Does He love me? Am I being punished for something?"

As I sat in the bleachers watching a football game one day, I heard a little boy exclaim to his mother, "I can see the bad guys more gooder than I can see the good guys!" Sometimes it may seem that we too can see the bad guys "more gooder" than we can see the good guys. I'm sure many of us have felt this way at some time. When we do, what is our reaction? It is sad that we often blame and even turn our backs on the only One who can help us. God says in Romans 12:21, "Do not be overcome by evil, but overcome evil with good."

It is beyond my comprehension to understand why these things happen. This I do know, however, Satan wants to destroy, but God is there to love and restore. It is through the difficult places, the frustrations, the trials, and, yes, even the tragedies that God wants to teach us more about Himself and build a stronger character within us. There is a saying, "The same sun that melts ice hardens clay." We can allow ourselves to become hard and bitter in our sufferings, or we can let God do a very special work in us. To every hurting person I would like to say that God is faithful. He knows, He cares, and He loves you. Trust Him! Trust Him! Trust Him!

The Lighthouse

There is an old worn lighthouse
Along a rugged shore.
It sets against a bleak gray sky
While waves below it roar.

The wind is cold and raging,
It whips about the sea,
While large and churning waves arise
To threaten one lone tree.

The night begins to hasten.
All is bleak and bare.
Then suddenly a light appears
To warm the chilly air.

It's from the old worn lighthouse.
How welcome is that light!
It shows the way to reach the shore
For those out in the night.

And so when life is sometimes
In total disarray,
When the storm is raging 'round us,
And we have lost our way;

It is then we see a beacon
That shines into the night.
It gives us hope when we are lost
And sets our lives aright.

This beacon light is Jesus.
He's there to show the way,
And every lost and wandering soul
Can find His help today.

Chapter 2

When You're Low and Still Sinking

Sitting on the davenport in our living room, I slid down far enough to rest my head against the back, stretched my feet out in front of me, and sighed deeply. It took more energy than I had to move, so I sat listless, just thinking and staring off into space. All of the painful events of the past few weeks ground their way through my mind, surfacing one by one into my thinking.

Where was our teenage daughter? What was she doing? What could make a loving, caring child turn into a bitter, angry person who said she hated both us and God?

Why had my husband just been fired? Hadn't his boss given him the leadership of one of the biggest projects in his department? Hadn't he just been commended for the good job he was doing and been given a raise?

Why did my body ache with pain day after day, hampering my ability to function as a wife and mother?

As I thought about these things, I knew God was real. He had proven Himself faithful many times, and any questions about His reality had been settled in my mind years before. I also knew that I was His child and that the Bible was full of wonderful promises that I personally could claim. I knew I could pray and God would hear my prayers, but somehow I couldn't get my heart to grasp what my mind was telling me. It was all vague and unreal. At that moment I needed a special touch from Him, a little something extra to renew the assurance of His love.

My mother has a calendar that says, "Reach up as far as you can.

God will reach down the rest of the way." I wasn't capable of reaching up very far that day, but God was very capable of reaching down.

I finally prayed a very simple prayer. I said, "Lord, I need something special from You today." That was it. There was not even an "Amen." As I said these words, I stood up and turned around. There it was, God's "something special" to me. Behind our davenport, a bay window held a number of plants, including a prayer plant. There on my prayer plant was a single, tiny, lavender flower. I had watered and cared for this plant for years. It had never bloomed—until that day!

I am convinced God sent that beautiful flower exactly when I needed it in answer to my prayer. By that little blossom I was reminded how much God cares about His creation, even to the smallest detail of a little flower. I knew He loved me much more than that flower, and that He would also take care of the most minute details of my life.

God knew how to reach me that day, and He caused my head knowledge to become heartfelt knowledge. How appropriate that this "answer to prayer" should bloom on my prayer plant. It blossomed continuously for the next three months and was a tangible, visible demonstration to me of God's love.

There may be times in our lives when we feel numb to spiritual reality, but I am glad God's faithfulness does not depend on how we feel. He may not always choose to give us tangible evidence of His love, but we can be confident in the fact of His love. God gives us a promise in 2 Corinthians 12:9 that says, "My grace is sufficient for you, for my power is made perfect in weakness." The Living Bible puts it this way, "...I am with you; that is all you need. My power shows up best in weak people."

When our burdens and cares seem so heavy we are not sure how we will make it, God says, "I am all you need." What a wonderful promise!

My Grace is Sufficient for Thee

Taken from 2 Corinthians 12:9 (KJ)

When trials are more than you can bear,
When darkness is all you can see,
Be still and listen to His voice,
"My grace is sufficient for thee."

When you don't understand the "whys" of life,
The reason things have to be,
He'll say, "Just trust in Me my child,
My grace is sufficient for thee."

Then we will learn when trials come,
When from life we want to flee,
He'll always be there and He will say,
"My grace is sufficient for thee."

Chapter 3

Black Pepper!

Our oldest son, Kevin, enjoys cooking. When he was about ten years old, we left him at home one day while we went to do some errands. While we were gone, he decided to surprise us by making a cake. The cake was in the oven baking when we arrived home, and the house smelled with the delicious aroma of the cake. We were very proud of him. Curious to know how he had gotten along, I asked him if he had encountered any problems while mixing the cake. He said there was only one. He couldn't figure out why the cake needed black pepper. In writing down the recipe, I had abbreviated the ingredient baking powder with the initials B.P. After investigating everything in the cupboard to find something with those initials, black pepper was the only thing he could find. Mixed with black pepper instead of baking powder, the cake smelled good, but it certainly did not taste good, and we had to throw it out.

Spiritually speaking, we may sometimes try to make substitutions for a personal relationship with Jesus Christ. We may substitute others who claim to be the way to eternal life, we may substitute good works, or we may just hope that things will work out when the time comes. Substitutions, however, don't work. We need the real thing. Jesus said in John 14:6, "I am the way and the truth and the life. No one comes to the Father except through me."

This personal relationship to Jesus Christ is vital if we are to be victorious in our suffering. We may have friends who love and pray for us, but Jesus is the only one who can bring the peace to our hearts that we so desperately need. Philippians 4:6-7 tells us, "Do not be anxious about anything, but in everything, by prayer and petition, with thanksgiving, present your requests to God. And the peace of God, which transcends all understanding, will guard your hearts and your minds in Christ Jesus." Nothing else will work. There is no substitute.

How do we find this road to peace, this relationship with Jesus Christ? First we must recognize that we are born in sin. Romans 5:12 (Liv) explains this reality. "When Adam sinned, sin entered the entire human race. His sin spread death throughout all the world so everything began to grow old and die, for all sinned."

If we stop here, we will despair, for sin separates us from a Holy God. Not only is this a physical death but a spiritual death. Jesus Christ, however, came to earth and gave Himself as the sacrifice for our sin by dying on a cross. In three days He arose from the grave, conquered death, went to heaven where He now intercedes for us, and He makes the gift of eternal life available to each one of us. 1 John 5:11-12 says, "And this is the testimony: God has given us eternal life, and this life is in His Son. He who has the Son has life; he who does not have the Son of God does not have life."

We see by these two verses that there are only two choices in life. We either have life in the Son of God or we do not. There is no middle road or substitute. We are free to choose our master. Being born in sin, we will be left in sin if no decision is made to do differently. To follow Jesus Christ means to believe in Him as our Savior and to confess our sins. It means opening our heart's door and inviting Him in to be our Lord.

I remember the first time I approached the concept of inviting Jesus into our hearts with our granddaughter Maria. She was still quite young and had climbed up on the davenport to look out of our big bay window. As she stood staring up at the beautiful expanse of sky with its galaxy of stars and bright full moon, she asked who had made the moon and stars. For the next few minutes I told her how God had created them and how He had also made her, and because He loved her, He wanted to come and live in her heart. After running around the house to confirm that everyone had a heart and to listen

18

to their heartbeats, she came running back and announced, "I want two hearts, one for God and one for Jesus and I want God to make them purple!" It was a beautiful thought.

As Christ takes up residency in our lives, a beautiful thing happens. We are made clean before God as if we had never sinned. 1 John 1:9 says, "If we confess our sins, He is faithful and just and will forgive us our sins and purify us from all unrighteousness."

It is wonderful to remember that I am no longer held guilty for sins I have confessed. They are forgiven and forgotten. Suffering may thus be a consequence, but never a punishment for past sins. Psalm 103:10-12 says, "He does not treat us as our sins deserve or repay us according to our iniquities. For as high as the heavens are above the earth, so great is His love for those who fear Him; as far as the east is from the west, so far has He removed our transgressions from us."

Even though I am God's child, as long as I am on this earth I will have suffering. I do not, however, have to live in defeat, for Jesus Christ will always be there to walk with me.

In Psalm 18:2 He gives us a wonderful promise. "The LORD is my rock, my fortress and my deliverer; my God is my rock, in whom I take refuge. He is my shield and the horn of my salvation, my stronghold." He is everything I will ever need.

In John 14:27 He also promises to give us peace. "Peace I leave with you; my peace I give you. I do not give to you as the world gives. Do not let your hearts be troubled and do not be afraid.

Neither do I need to doubt His love, or wonder if He has forsaken me. He gives us this comforting message in Hebrews 13:5b, "Never will I leave you; never will I forsake you."

Black pepper may be good on steak, but it certainly is not good in cake. Some of our substitutions may sound good, but the end result is disastrous! Jesus Christ is the only way to eternal life, and He is the only one who can give us the help we need to get through our trials. There is no substitute!

No Substitutions

Substitutions may sound good,
And we may try a few.
But if we want eternal life,
There's only one way through.

This only way is Jesus.
He died that we might live.
He's promised us eternal life
If Him our hearts we give.

He took upon Himself our sins.
How marvelous such love!
He's now preparing each of us
A place in heaven above.

And when I reach the other side
And see that promised land,
I'll not remember suffering here
For He will take my hand.

This is my hope, this is my joy,
To see His face some day.
For He has promised He Himself
Will wipe all tears away.

Then I will walk those golden streets,
And golden bells will ring.
In triumph and in victory
With angels I will sing!

No, there are no substitutions,
Christ is the only way;
And He Himself will welcome me
When I go home some day.

Chapter 4

Broken Pieces

"Humpty Dumpty sat on a wall,
Humpty Dumpty had a great fall.
All the king's horses and all the king's men
Could not put Humpty together again."

When our daughter Sheryl left home at the age of eighteen and got involved with drugs, alcohol, and sex, there were times when I thought she too was broken and shattered beyond repair. Her life seemed a total shambles of disarray and confusion. Our relationship through the years had been good and there were many happy memories. What had happened?

With Sheryl's permission, I share her story.

It began the day she left home. It was beyond my comprehension that she could pack up and leave without a word. Even worse was the fact that she was leaving with her boyfriend. Was she planning to live with him? He lived with his parents. Surely they wouldn't allow that to happen, but they did. I was furious! Because they were of age, however, we were helpless to do anything. We could only pray, and pray we did!

We knew we also needed others to pray, but we were very hesitant to call anyone. What would people think? We soon swallowed our pride and fears, however, and called some praying people. It was the best decision we could have made.

During the months that followed, my husband Shelly and I spent many sleepless nights in prayer. Drinking and drugs were involved, but we had no idea how much. To find peace, I had to get my eyes off the circumstances and on to Jesus Christ. As one friend said, "Remember! God will only allow in her life that which will bring her back to Him." I often envisioned angels around her in a circle of protection, and I believed God was working in her life even though I couldn't see it happening.

Gradually, as communication improved between us, we learned that Sheryl was sexually molested by a trusted friend as she was growing up. I know she tried to tell us, but she wasn't sure what to say, and we weren't getting the message. We understand now that she was angry at both God and us for not protecting her. Her questions were, "Where was God? Where were my parents? Why did this happen to me?"

We continually assured Sheryl of our love and desire for her to come home, but we also made it clear we would never compromise our standards to condone her lifestyle. In the next few months she moved in and out of our home four times. Each time she left, she would disappear without a word.

During this time we were living a nightmare, torn between hope and despair. There was the nightmare of a telephone call in the early hours of the morning. Sheryl and her friends were hiding from her boyfriend. They were waiting for him with a gun. He also had a gun and was looking for her. She would not say where she was. She just wanted us to know.

"Oh, Lord, please protect our daughter!" He did.

There was the nightmare of attempted suicide when the doctor said that if the pills she had swallowed were in her stomach longer than forty-five minutes, there could be permanent damage. They were there one and a half hours.

"Oh, Lord, please protect our daughter!" He did.

There was the nightmare of her boyfriend holding a gun to his head and threatening suicide unless she came to him. We were afraid he might kill them both.

"Oh, Lord, please protect our daughter!" He did.

How many times were the policemen at our door? How many

times did we fear for her life? How many times did we cry? How many times did we hope? I don't know. Only God knows all the details of those days.

A verse that became very meaningful to me at this time was Isaiah 61:3: "To bestow on them (her) a crown of beauty instead of ashes, the oil of gladness instead of mourning, and a garment of praise instead of a spirit of despair. They will be called oaks of righteousness, a planting of the Lord for the display of his splendor."

Think of it! When there are only ashes, there aren't even any pieces to put together! Soot and dust disintegrate to the touch and blow away in the wind, but He restores the ashes to something beautiful. I prayed, "Lord, this is what you promised and this is what I am believing for Sheryl."

I wrote out this verse and other verses and put them on the refrigerator, on her pictures, and in various places around the house. I filled my mind with God's promises so there wouldn't be any room for doubts, putting the word "TRUST!" in big letters across the refrigerator.

The following years have been difficult ones for Sheryl. Breaking up with her boyfriend, she heard a young man give his testimony about how God had saved him out of alcohol and drugs. She decided if God could do that for him, He could do the same for her. As a result, she decided to walk with God and, as she said later, "I sincerely gave my heart to Christ for the first time." She and this young man started dating and in a few months were married.

The honeymoon, however, was brief. After three years of marriage and the arrival of a beautiful baby daughter, her husband was killed in a tragic house fire. Sheryl's emotions were shattered, and again there was the struggle of being able to trust God with her life. Thank God for loving Christians who were not judgmental but totally accepting of Sheryl.

Since that time Sheryl has had another little girl and has lost a second husband also in a tragic death. However, it is encouraging to know that no matter how bad things are, we are never out of God's reach. Telling her story of being in a concentration camp, Corrie Ten

Boom said, "No pit is so deep that He is not deeper still."

Gradually the fact that God does love her and has a plan for her is becoming a reality to Sheryl. She is once again finding the joy and peace God gives as she yields herself into His keeping. God is healing the hurts and continues to put the broken pieces back together. We just keep praying and hanging on to God to "complete the work He has started" in her life. Someday we'll be able to say that He has made "beauty out of the ashes."

A Sunrise

The sky was gray and all was still
As night broke into day.
Then softly shades of pink arose
On horizons far away.

I watched in joy and wonder
To see the sun arise,
As gradually the pink turned rose
And spread across the skies.

The hues were pretty to behold.
I stood there full of awe;
And then the sun itself appeared,
A round, red rim I saw.

Then gradually the sky turned red
And orange and purple too.
With colors bright across the sky,
Day had begun anew.

I felt all good and right inside,
All yesterdays behind.
And now I looked ahead to see
What new things I could find.

For my life was shattered pieces
Until God's power came.
Then He made something beautiful,
Removing all my shame.

Yes, the past is all behind me.
Today is a new day!
I'll live it knowing that my God
Will help me on my way.

And when the sun sets in the west,
This day is lived and done,
I'll start anew, afresh tomorrow
With the rising of the sun.

Chapter 5

Why Trials, Anyway!

A question every one of us will probably ask sometime in our life and one of the hardest we will ever have to answer is, "Why must I have trials and suffering?" We will probably never fully understand all of God's purposes for suffering, but there are some things that might give us insights into this question.

We need to be careful not to confuse trials with temptations. James 1:13-14 says, "When tempted, no one should say, 'God is tempting me.' For God cannot be tempted by evil, nor does he tempt anyone; but each one is tempted when, by his own evil desire, he is dragged away and enticed." Yielding to temptation always leads to destruction.

However, God sometimes allows trials to help us grow. A trial is a test. If we look at "trial" in one of the definitions of Webster's Dictionary, we read, "It helps us grow in quality and usefulness by means of tribulation, affliction, and suffering." It is this definition that gives suffering a purpose and makes it valuable as we yield our suffering to God.

A doctor friend kept a paraphrase of Romans 8:28 in his office that read, "The Lord may not have planned that this should overtake me, but He has most certainly permitted it. Therefore though it were an attack of an enemy, by the time it reaches me, it has the Lord's permission and therefore all is well. He will make it work together with all life's experiences for good."

I am reminded of a football coach that our son Greg had in junior high school. Sometimes his techniques seemed a little rough, and the boys complained a lot. One day when I was talking to this coach, he said, "I am interested in more than winning. I do things that will help teach these kids responsibility so they will someday develop into responsible young men."

As I understood this, my perspective of the game changed, and I had a new appreciation for the hard work required of the team. Their coach had a future goal in mind. He wanted them to be the best they could be.

Sometimes life may get rough for us, too, and we may be prone to complain. But our Head Coach, Jesus Christ, sees something we don't. As we learn to trust Him, He will work out His purpose and plan for us and gradually fashion and shape us to be a usable vessel for Him. He, too, wants us to be the best we can be.

As Greg was growing up, he had several things that were trials for him. He was one of the smallest boys in his class at school. Also, he had to wear glasses, and his teeth needed braces. As our third child, he was sure all of the "good stuff" had already gone into his brother and sister, and he felt he was put together with the "leftovers." He thought he would never grow or amount to anything.

But something happened through the years. As he grew older, he developed into a well-built, handsome young man. He wears contacts when he chooses, his teeth are attractive, and everyone in our house has to look up to him as the tallest one in the family!

Greg was also a strong-willed child with a temper to match. His exasperated teacher at school would call saying Greg had just kicked over a chair and run from the classroom, or he had stubbornly decided he was not going to do something that he was told to do. Not very long ago Greg said to me, "I don't know what I will do if I ever get a child like me."

"What do you mean?" I asked.

"I know how difficult I could be to reason with at times," he answered. "I know how I sometimes argued and only wanted my own way."

Greg has grown up, both physically and perceptively. He now understands our love and concerns for him and can much better understand why we as parents did what we did. He has learned that because we love him, he can trust us to help him become the best he can be.

This is the way we should grow in our love toward God. As we continually see God working, see His love that never fails, and feel His presence in our lives, we learn more and more to let go and trust Him to run our lives. We learn to look beyond our own desires, knowing He has a higher, better plan for us.

Looking again at Romans 8:28 in the NIV, we read, "And we know that in all things God works for the good of those who love Him, who have been called according to His purpose."

Sometimes God's idea of what is good for me may be very different than my idea of what is good for me. One day our oldest son Kevin said, "Hey, Mom! I see we don't have any good bananas in the house." My immediate response was, "Yes we do, Kevin. There's a bunch of good bananas in the cupboard." Then I realized Kevin's definition of good was very different than mine. To me, good bananas meant those that were not overly ripe, but to him, good bananas meant those that were very ripe. A child's definition for good may be eating ice cream and cake for dinner instead of vegetables and fruit, and not understanding our reasoning, they may cry to get it.

Why do we have trials? I need to remember that an all knowing and loving God knows far better than I what I need in my life to help me become the person He wants me to be. As we remember the definition for trial in the beginning of this chapter, we know that tribulation, affliction and suffering help us grow in quality and usefulness for Jesus Christ. We may never fully understand God's purposes, but we must believe that God is God, and in so doing, we must let God be God, for His way is perfect.

Christ is the Potter

Christ is the potter. I'm the clay.
He gently takes a hold
And lifts me up within His hands
And starts to shape and mold.

He has a picture in His mind
Of just what I will be
When He has finished with His work
And He is done with me.

He puts me on the wheel of life,
I turn and spin around
While He so gently works and shapes
To smooth the lumps He's found.

But I'm unyielding, hard to change,
As stubborn as can be.
I often slow His work, but He
Just works on patiently.

Just when I think I'm finally done,
I'm placed into the fire.
But it's then that I am usable,
And that is His desire.

Sometimes I think that I know best
And want to try my way.
But I just always mess things up
When from His hands I stray.

So gradually I learn to yield
And let Him fashion me.
For He's the potter and will make
Of me what I should be.

So make me usable, dear Lord,
This vessel made of clay.
Shaped and fashioned by Your hand
And yielded every day.

Chapter 6

An Unusual God

Kathryn's Story:

"We had four beautiful children, and although our second child, Johnny, looked perfectly normal at birth, at three years of age it was discovered that he had brain damage."

Kathryn sat across the table from me as she shared her story. As she talked, my mind went back many years. Linda, their oldest, and I had been best friends, and I had been in their home many times. I also knew Johnny and their other children Karolyn and Paul. This family had a strong faith in God that had brought them through many difficulties, and I anticipated hearing Kathryn's story.

"I was sixteen before I heard the claims of Christ on my life," Kathryn explained. "I thought if you went to church and tried to live right, you were okay. Then a retired minister came and held revival services. Since I was the church pianist, I was there at every meeting. It was then that I learned what it means to be a Christian, and I accepted Christ into my life.

"When I was eighteen, I went to college where I met John. He had a beautiful tenor voice and sang in a quartet. When he moved with the quartet to another state to work and travel in special meetings, I left school a couple of months later to join him and get married.

"When we had Johnny and discovered he had brain damage, it was very traumatic. I remember having seen a retarded boy one time and saying, 'One thing I could never stand is to have a child like that.' The Lord showed me I could stand it.

"The brain damage was caused because the doctor was an alcoholic, and the birth was delayed unnecessarily. The nurses had been instructed to give me ether, and when I started having contractions, they clamped an ether can over my face. He should have been born hours sooner than he was. Both of us were damaged by too much ether.

"It was definitely a struggle to forgive that doctor. I had already had a series of miscarriages, and this doctor had encouraged me to keep trying again. He kept assuring me that I should be able to have another healthy baby. Then it was he who caused so much grief by not being there when I needed him. I carried a great burden of resentment toward him. I knew I had to get over that.

"Then I read Hannah Whiteall Smith's book entitled, *The Christian's Secret of a Happy Life.* She wrote about accepting what the Lord allows in one's life. God had not necessarily caused it or planned for it to happen, but He had allowed it to happen. Therefore I had to say, 'Lord, You allowed this for a purpose. Now if You'll just show me what the purpose is, I would like to fulfill it to the very end of my life and to the extent of my energy.' God has privileged both my husband and me to use this experience in helping many people who have had similar experiences. When I gained this perspective on things, a burden rolled off my back. I had to realize that letting that hurt fester and not getting it out in the open and really forgiving the doctor was just damaging my family and me. I had become obsessed with it. I had to make a choice to forgive.

"I can't say the hurt is gone. It is still there, mainly because I think of Johnny's potential. He is autistic (absorbed in fantasy to the exclusion of interest in reality) and doesn't talk much, but he understands most of what he is told and is very musical. He has perfect pitch and knows the tune and words of everything he hears. He would have been a terrific musician if he would have had the other mental faculties to develop his talent.

"John is in a hospital school now. When we go to see him, we hear all sorts of rock music coming out of the rooms. I'm sure he doesn't hear much sacred music, but when we take Johnny for a ride, we say, 'Sing us a song, Johnny.' He always sings 'Jesus Loves Me,' which is one of the songs he learned at home. Since he was eleven years old when he left our home and is forty-two now, it has been a long time since he has heard that song.

"This is encouraging because if he remembers that and associates it with home, then a child who is brought up in a Christian home can't ever forget what he has learned. It must have an influence on him no matter how he may try to get away from it. I have told Christian parents despairing of a child who wants to go the wrong way to just hang on. It may be difficult, but God will remind him of how he ought to go.

"As a family we always pray for Johnny. At first we prayed that he would get well. Then we gradually tempered our prayers and accepted the fact that he wasn't going to get well. I think it increased our faith and helped us all to trust the Lord. His way is best even when we don't agree."

Other heartaches and trials that Kathryn shared with me that day included the loss of their baby Helene, learning to live with the pain and limitations of rheumatoid arthritis, her husband John's having a heart attack, and the loss of their home in a flood. In each situation God has given them the strength they have needed to carry on.

A favorite scripture that has helped Kathryn through her trials is Psalm 91. To quote the first few verses, "He who dwells in the shelter of the Most High will rest in the shadow of the Almighty. I will say of the Lord, 'He is my refuge and my fortress, my God, in whom I trust.' Surely He will save you from the fowler's snare and from the deadly pestilence. He will cover you with His feathers, and under His wings you will find refuge; His faithfulness will be your shield and rampart."

When I told Kathryn I could see a Christ-like spirit in her, her comment was, "Thank you. That's the most important thing to me. I don't want anything I do to call attention to me or make it seem that I'm an unusual person. I have an unusual God, that's all."

I Met With Him This Morning

This day is very special
For Christ is by my side.
I met with Him this morning.
He said He'd be my guide.

And so whatever this day brings,
He'll be right there with me.
I know He'll work things for my good
No matter what they be.

I pray that those I meet today
Will see His love through me,
That I will be so close to Him
His glory they will see.

And may I help another find
Real peace sent from above,
That they will also know this friend
Who guides me with His love.

Chapter 7

The Value of Gold

Job 23:10 declares, "But He knows the way that I take; when He has tested me, I will come forth as gold." Gold is precious and it is attractive. Is it any wonder that God allows testing in our lives if it brings us forth as gold?

To make gold more valuable, it has to be refined with a high temperature to remove the impurities and reduce it to a pure state. The purer the gold, the more beautiful and valuable it becomes.

Because we are valuable to God, He also takes us through a refining process to remove the impurities in our lives. When I was in college, our campus had many beautiful trees which became infested with little worms. The worms hung from the trees on a web, which I often would not see until I had walked into it. After walking into a worm a few times, I could no longer enjoy the beautiful trees. I was too busy looking for the worms!

As we allow God to refine and purify us, He removes all of the little "worms" in our lives that keep the attention of others on us instead of on His beauty in us. As He does so, others will see less of self and more of Christ.

Some of the most useful and beautiful objects of the world are made from gold. Its softness makes it very workable, allowing it to be shaped into any form.

So also God would like to fashion and shape us into His masterpiece, special and unique from all others. The more impurities God removes, the easier we will be for God to work with. As we become soft and pliable in His hands, He can more and more shape us into a beautiful, usable vessel filled more and more with Himself to be used for His purposes.

When gold is to be made into a hard object, such as a piece of jewelry, it must be combined with some other metal to make it strong and durable. Such a mixture is called an alloy.

We need God as our alloy. Without Him we will not have the strength and resistance we need to withstand the pressures of the world and the attacks of Satan.

Finally, gold can be thinned down so that it becomes translucent. It is then applied to glass and can be used for windows.

We too need to become translucent, that those looking through the window of our lives may clearly see Jesus Christ.

Since we are human, it is sometimes quite hard to leave the refining process to God to work out as He pleases. I'm afraid that all too often we try to dictate the pattern of God's shaping process, forgetting who is the Master. Are we willing to let Him be the Master, to be just exactly what He wants us to be? Are we willing to be refined by the fire so that we can shine as pure gold?

As valuable as gold is, God says our faith is even more valuable to Him. 1 Peter 1:7 (Living) states, "These trials are only to test your faith, to see whether or not it is strong and pure. It is being tested as fire tests gold and purifies it—and your faith is far more precious to God than mere gold; so if your faith remains strong after being tried in the test tube of fiery trials, it will bring you much praise and glory and honor on the day of His return."

We were in the Black Hills of South Dakota one summer taking a tour of a gold mine. We had learned many interesting things about mining gold, and now I stood looking at the finished product. "Is this all there is?" I exclaimed in unbelief. All of the hours of work involved to extract and process the gold from one ton of dirt had resulted in a piece of gold the size of a chocolate chip.

It really didn't matter, however, how much work and time was involved in digging and processing the gold. It was the value of the finished product that mattered, and the little piece of gold I was looking at was very valuable.

God is interested in the finished product. The process may be long and difficult, but He wants us to come forth as pure gold, precious and attractive to a world lost in sin that they too might come to know Jesus Christ as Lord and Savior.

Make Me Usable, Dear Lord

Am I willing to be exactly
What He wants me to be?
To trust myself into His care
Though His plan I cannot see?

I'm far more precious in His sight
Than purest, finest gold.
So I'll let Him be the master
And let Him shape and mold.

He'll take out my impurities
And refine me with fire.
To make me something usable
Is His plan and desire.

As I then become translucent,
His love through me will flow
To reach a dying world for Christ
That His love they may know.

Yes, make me usable, dear Lord,
Wherever that may be.
Refined and purified as gold,
That I many shine for Thee.

Chapter 8

Though Blind, I See

Marion's Story:

"I was a premature baby, weighing two pounds fourteen ounces, and so spent the first three months of my life in an incubator," Marion shares. "Because the oxygen level was too high, my eyes were damaged. To my recollection, I was blind in one eye and legally blind in the other.

"As I grew up, I spent days and days at the eye doctor. Wearing glasses helped a little. When I looked across the room I could see the outline of a person and the colors he was wearing, but I couldn't distinctly see the face. I could also read, but the print had to be large and very close to my face.

"I accepted the Lord when I was five years old. After Sunday School one day, I went home, knelt down in my bedroom, and prayed. I felt so cleansed! I can still remember the blue painted walls and the white ceiling of that room.

"I did a lot of singing in high school. Because of my eye problem, life was a struggle, and I sang a lot of songs about suffering and trials. I was also burdened to memorize scripture and to put large portions of it away in my heart. I remember lying on the living room floor, poring over my large print Bible. I had such a love for His Word. I could never seem to get enough of it.

"I am so thankful I memorized all I did because I can no longer read for myself. I never prepared to be totally blind because my eye doctor thought my vision would probably remain the same throughout my life. God knew, however, I needed that preparation, and now those verses come back over and over again at times when I really need them. It's wonderful.

"I met Richard when I was in high school. When he asked me to marry him, I brought up the fact that I only had one eye. I asked, 'What if something happens to that eye?' Richard's immediate response was, 'That's no problem to me. It would be an honor for me to be the eyes for our family.' After much prayer, however, we both knew we should not marry.

"One day while I was teaching school, my fourth graders suddenly became very blurry. By the time I got home, all I could see was a big, white glob where my house was, and I was in excruciating pain. It was glaucoma. In all of those years, my eye doctor had never tested me for glaucoma.

"I saw my eye doctor the next day. He gave me some medicine and kept saying that it would be okay. Eventually, however, he took the medicine away. This caused my eye to hemorrhage internally, thus doing further damage. Since that time I have not even had light perception.

"At that time there was a peace I cannot understand or explain. There was nothing I could do except trust God to work and guide in my life. I'm not saying there were no frustrations. There were many, but God's peace was there in a very real way.

"It was after I lost my eyesight that Richard proposed again. Now God's timing was perfect. If we would have gotten married before that, I would have spent the rest of my life feeling that Richard was stuck with me. This way he accepted me the way I was and still wanted and loved me. How thankful I am that both of us followed God's leading even though we didn't understand.

"Richard and my supervisor agreed that I should teach school again, so I went back in the fall to the same children I had taught before. They were my eyes, my helpers, and everything. I depended greatly upon my ears and had a seating chart, so I knew who was sitting where. One day I heard a boy playing with his pen. I looked toward him and said, 'Jeff, put your pen away, please.' The kids were ecstatic. They thought I could see again.

"God prepared a very special man for me. How blessed I am to have a husband who reads the Bible to me, prays with me, and reads Christian books to me. He has taught me how to cook and how to do crafts. We basically do everything together. This has been a real bonding factor in our marriage. I always tell young people to let God choose their mate. He will do an absolutely perfect job.

"We have fun times together, too. One winter Richard and I went to bed early to read. A friend called and wanted to borrow some flour, so we decided that I would go downstairs to get it. Richard said, 'Honey, please don't forget to turn the lights on,' so I turned the lights on outside, in the hallway, and in the living room. When my friend got into the kitchen, I handed her the scoop, telling her to get what she needed. As I did, she stammered, 'Uh, well, uh.' I said, 'What's wrong?' She said, 'Well, I'm not used to doing this in the dark!' I had forgotten to turn the kitchen light on!

"After I lost my sight, I quit singing. I felt that someday God was going to restore my sight in a miraculous way, and when He did, I would burst into song again. God has given me the ability, however, to accept the fact that if I will not see here on earth, I will see in heaven. Thanks to a pastor I call the 'Gentle Bulldozer' and to the nudging of the Lord, I'm singing again.

"I have a prayer group that meets in my home once a week, and I also pray with people who are hurting. My new and exciting venture is holding Bible studies with new Christians. My pastor's wife recorded the lessons on cassette so I could learn them and be able to teach them. I especially like to teach the children.

"I know it's because of the Lord that I'm able to still have joy in my heart in spite of my sufferings and losses in life. My favorite verse is Isaiah 41:10 (KJ). 'Fear thou not for I am with thee: be not dismayed; for I am thy God: I will strengthen thee; yea, I will help thee; yea, I will uphold thee with the right hand of my righteousness.' I have needed the Lord's strength very much, and I have been fearful, yet He tells me not to be, and He helps me walk through those dark places where I cannot see.

"Richard and I also share some favorite verses. Proverbs 3:5-6 (King James) says, 'Trust in the Lord with all thine heart; and lean not unto thine own understanding. In all thy ways acknowledge Him, and He shall direct thy paths.' We really don't understand God's ways, but we need to trust, rest, and acknowledge Him, and He will direct us. The Lord has been so good and so precious. I can even thank Him for my blindness because when I could not see others, I could see Him. I know that through this I have gotten to know Him in a closer, deeper way, and it has been wonderful."

Here Am I, Use Me

Now we may think that in this life
We've nothing we can give
To really count in serving God
As day to day we live.

But it really doesn't matter
Who we think that we may be.
It's what God thinks that really counts
And availability.

For, God, You used a fisherman,
A tax collector, too.
The blind, the lame, the rich, the poor,
It matters not to You.

So whatever You may choose for me,
Whether great or small,
You made me with a special plan,
Just help me give my all.

And though my talents may seem few,
Available I'll be.
A vessel to be used of God,
Yes, here am I, use me!

Chapter 9

Ouch! It Hurts!

Shopping for groceries one day, I saw a little girl giving her grandmother a very difficult time. It seemed that whatever the grandmother told the little girl to do, she was doing just the opposite. Her little face was all smiles while being deliberately naughty and watching her grandmother's reactions to her antics. Suddenly, the grandmother reached over and gave the little girl a swat. Immediately, her attitude changed. Her smiling face turned tearful, and her disobedient spirit changed to obedience. Her grandmother did not have any more trouble with her.

When the Israelites grumbled and disbelieved God, He disciplined them. From Deuteronomy 8:2-5 we read, "Remember how the Lord your God led you all the way in the desert these forty years, to humble you and to test you in order to know what was in your heart, whether or not you would keep His commands. He humbled you, causing you to hunger and then feeding you with manna, which neither you nor your fathers had known, to teach you that man does not live on bread alone but on every word that comes from the mouth of the Lord. Your clothes did not wear out and your feet did not swell during these forty years. Know then in your heart that as a man disciplines his son, so the Lord your God disciplines you."

When God disciplined the Israelites, He still took care of their needs. Although they did not enjoy steak dinners with potatoes and a rich dessert while in the desert, God gave them manna. Neither did they go shopping for new clothes and new shoes for forty years. The ones they had did not wear out!

God never stopped loving the Israelites when He disciplined them just as the grandmother's love never stopped toward her granddaughter when she gave her a swat. God proved His continued love and care for the Israelites all of those years while they were in the desert.

As the grandmother wanted a change in behavior, so God also gives us discipline with a purpose in mind. I have a friend who had some extensive remodeling done at her house. There were three boys living at home, and the only living space available on the main floor was two bedrooms and a bath which were very crowded with things brought in from the other rooms. The kitchen, living room, and another bedroom were full of boards, sawdust, carpenters, and the noise of hammers and saws. She and her family lived the best they could in the basement.

My friend knew the end product would be beautiful, but the transition from the old to the new was very difficult. Knowing, however, that all of the difficulty she was going through would be worth it in the end, she stayed encouraged.

James 1:2-4 says, "Consider it pure joy, my brothers, whenever you face trials of many kinds, because you know that the testing of your faith develops perseverance. Perseverance must finish its work so that you may be mature and complete, not lacking anything."

Many of us have heard the saying, "Please be patient. God isn't finished with me yet." God is gradually transforming us from the old person we used to be to the new person He wants us to become. Sometimes the changes are hard, and He has to hammer or saw away on our pride or stubbornness, or some other area He wants to change. As He continues to work, progress is gradually made.

Whatever the reason God chooses to discipline us, we have the assurance He will continue to love and take care of us, and that there will always be a purpose. We may want to holler, "Ouch! It hurts!" but someday when He has finished His work, He will take us home, perfect and beautiful. Then we will know that any "remodeling" He has done on us here will be worth it all there.

From Worm to Butterfly

A tiny golden butterfly
Floats gently through the air,
To land on flowers one by one
And suck the nectar there.

A caterpillar it once was
That crawled upon this earth,
Until it spun a small cocoon
And then it had new birth.

A new birth and a miracle,
From worm to butterfly.
A change that only God could make,
But old self had to die.

So we are only such as worms
That to ourselves must die.
And then God molds our life into
A golden butterfly.

Chapter 10

A God Of Miracles

Pat & Rhio's Story:

"As I did my inspection on the top of an elevator, a trap door gave way, and I fell through. I landed twelve feet below on a hard-surfaced floor. The results of that fall have been lasting. I broke my head, my back, my attitude, and a bunch of things, and it really changed our lives."

Rhio grew up in the depression years, leaving home at fourteen to work in a lead and silver mine. Seeing no future in that life, he went back home, worked long hard hours to put himself through college, got a good job, married, and had three children.

"I was proud of my accomplishments," Rhio shares, "and success became my God. It was my focus and purpose in life. The more I achieved, the more I wanted, and I was not afraid to exploit other people to make myself look good. Rising fast in a political party, I proudly wore the badge of my success. I knew all of the right people and was known in important social circles, being inducted into the Industrial Shrine Club the meeting before John Wayne was inducted. I had a good wife, three beautiful children, and a nice home.

"One day, however, I came home to find a U-Haul parked in my driveway. My wife was leaving me, and she was leaving the kids with me. At that point my whole world came tumbling down. I was no longer in control. My job no longer had a future, and the political and social circles that I had been so active in no longer needed me. I was being ignored, and that was one of the most devastating things that could have happened to me.

"With the upheaval of a couple of job changes and with single parenting for the next four years, I entered a deep depression. Then I met a lovely lady named Pat, and we went to a Billy Graham crusade. When the invitation was given, we both went forward and dedicated our lives to Christ. Six months later we were married. With Pat and I each having three children, it was quite an adjustment for all of us, but soon we merged as a happy family.

"Moving to Iowa, I enjoyed a job repairing elevators. I was still struggling with my independent attitude, knowing I belonged to God, but finding it hard to totally depend on Him. That is when I fell through the elevator. After that happened, I could no longer work and had to retire. For someone who had been an aggressive worker since the age of fourteen, this was a big adjustment!"

As Pat begins to share, she says, "We could immediately see God's hand in a number of areas that let us know He was with us through all of it. I was out of town when I learned that Rhio had fallen at work and had been taken to the hospital. The verse that came to me that morning was Psalm 37:23-24 (NAS) that says, 'The steps of a man are established by the Lord; and He delights in his way. When he falls, he shall not be hurled headlong; because the Lord is the One who holds his hand.'

When Rhio lost his balance and fell, he could have been hurled headlong over the side of the elevator ending up three stories below. Instead he went through the top and landed in the bottom of the elevator.

"We also saw God's hand in other ways. A Christian lady just 'happened' to be on the same elevator where Rhio fell, and he landed at her feet. She was so sure he was dead, she began praying immediately. From the moment he went through the top of the elevator God had one of His people there praying and taking care of him.

"When the ambulance came, the driver was a friend. For some reason I still don't know, he took Rhio to the hospital in the next town and our family doctor was already at the hospital. He knew the people to call in order to locate me.

"God also miraculously took care of our finances. We had bought a car and had made only two payments on it. Disability insurance was something completely foreign to me, yet we learned that we had it, and it completely paid for our car.

"We often didn't have the money to make payments that were due. One time when insurance, taxes, and house payments were all due at the same time, Rhio went to the bank and asked them to take our house back. We wanted to give it to them, but they wouldn't take it. We didn't know what to do, but money started coming in from some very unlikely sources, and we were able to pay our bills."

Rhio continues, "The recovery process took a long time. At first I couldn't walk very far. There was a signpost about a hundred yards from our house. It was a real glory day when I made it to the post and back without having to be steadied.

"I still get dizzy and have problems with vertigo, a spatial disorientation. There is no right side up or upside down. Nothing is true. Today, I still have to be very careful about lifting things, not only because I can hurt my back, but also because I get very dizzy.

"As I got better, my greatest decision was the direction I should go with my life. I prayed much about this. Having completed my Master's Degree just one month before my accident with the purpose of going into Christian counseling, I started counseling at church and calling on people in hospitals. I am on staff today as a counselor. I also have a radio program doing interviews with the pastors in the area. This has been an exciting opportunity!

"Three years ago, I started reading my Bible through each year. As a result, the Bible has really taken on new meaning and life for me. It wasn't because the people in the Bible were perfect that miracles were done, but because of God's faithfulness.

"One of the biggest things God has accomplished through all of this is the fact that I have had to let go of those areas I was still hanging on to and let God take the controls. Our goal in life is just to glorify God and to be used by Him."

I Asked to Find Real Happiness

I asked to find real happiness.
I looked and searched around.
I searched in wealth and precious stones,
But nothing there I found.

I thought that maybe lands or lakes
Or trees or ocean shore
Would help me find the special thing
That I was looking for.

I longed to rest my troubled heart,
To know real peace of mind.
I hoped that someday as I searched
A purpose I would find.

And then one day I found a hill,
A hill called Calvary.
I saw a cross and then I knew
That Christ had died for me.

I asked forgiveness for my sins,
And I found peace that day.
Christ gave my life a purpose
And I knew He was the way.

So if you're searching for new life,
For hope and peace of mind,
Kneel now before the cross of Christ,
And all these things you'll find.

Chapter 11

Painful Pruning

One day I was thumbing through an old ledger book of my mother's. "Mom, I can't believe you have all of this stuff written down!" I exclaimed. Suddenly I was reliving my life many years ago, a young girl growing up on a fruit ranch in Oregon. I could envision my mom and dad, my two sisters, and myself standing in one of the long rows of thick, green, boysenberry vines, filling our boxes full of big, purple, luscious fruit. I could also envision other fields where we had worked. There were fields of blackcaps and strawberries and the grove of filbert trees where we had picked the ripened nuts off the ground. In her ledger Mom had listed each of our names and the amount of pay we had received for our labors.

What I found even more interesting in the ledger, however, were the large amounts of fruit she had canned. For instance, the year 1949 read, Royal Anne Cherries—43 quarts; Lambert Cherries—24 quarts; Raspberries—2 quarts; Apricots—14 quarts; Boysenberries—68 quarts; Applesauce—43 quarts; Plums—11 quarts; Pears—83 quarts; Peaches—66 quarts; and Prunes—64 quarts, for a total of 448 quarts of fruit.

Besides all of the fruit, she had also canned 210 quarts of vegetables.

I was overwhelmed! "How did you ever can so much, and where did you get it all?" I asked.

"We gleaned the fields after the workers were done," she explained. "We were allowed to keep whatever we picked."

I thought about all of the fruit and all of the hard work required to grow and harvest that fruit. I also thought about the pruning required to produce good fruit.

In pruning, unwanted plant growth is cut and removed to make the plant grow and behave the proper way. This must be done for successful production and gives many benefits to the plant. It increases the percentage of top-grade fruit, increases the size of the fruit, decreases pre-harvest fruit drop, promotes tree vigor, reduces winter injury, and reduces limb breakage. Pruning also opens up the top of the tree to let in sunlight. This produces better fruit color and higher sugar content making the fruit sweeter and more flavorful.

Working on a fruit ranch, my dad learned how to prune grape vines. Often the branches of the vines were cut back so far that people thought they would surely die. The vines that were pruned, however, gave the greatest abundance of fruit. If the vines were not pruned correctly, they did not produce good fruit either in quality or quantity.

One day as I was reading my Bible, I read John 15:1-2. "I am the true vine, and my Father is the gardener. He cuts off every branch in me that bears no fruit, while every branch that does bear fruit he prunes so that it will be even more fruitful."

I had read this verse many times with the emphasis on cutting off every branch that bore no fruit. Suddenly, I was really seeing the second part of the verse that talks about the branch that does bear fruit. Even though it is already bearing fruit, the good branch has to be pruned so it can bear more fruit.

Wow! That hurts! When God prunes us, the purpose and benefits will be the same as with the fruit tree. He will remove unwanted growth of our lives that keep us from growing and behaving the way He desires. As we yield to His plan and purpose, we grow in faith, become stronger spiritually, and produce better fruit for Him. The pruning may be painful, but it is essential to our spiritual growth.

God's Garden

There is a special garden
With flowers everywhere.
These flowers are so beautiful,
They are so very rare.

The keeper of this garden
Knows every flower there.
He cuts and plants and prunes and trims
And gives them special care.

He knows each flower by its name.
He knows what makes each grow.
So some have sun and some have shade,
Each in a special row.

Now each of us are flowers, too
In God's great garden fair.
For in His garden we are placed
Within His loving care.

He knows what's best for each of us.
He shapes and trims and hoes.
He sends the sunshine and the rain.
A plan for each He knows.

So God allows us some of both,
Of rain and sunshine too.
Whatever helps us grow the best
Is just what He will do.

So know that you are special.
He tends you carefully.
Be beautiful and bloom for God
Wherever you may be.

Chapter 12

Battered and Bruised

Jeanne's Story:

"The earliest recollection I have of abuse was when I was about three years old," shares Jeanne. "My parents sent me to my bedroom. I locked the door, climbed into my crib, and went to sleep. The next thing I remember was my dad screaming and taking the door off the hinges. He grabbed me, threw me under his arm, and carried me down the steps to the basement. I was petrified! He beat me with a razor strap, hauled me back up the steps, and threw me into my crib.

"My dad beat all of my brothers. He broke a leather razor strap on one of their backs. He always screamed "hell and brimstone" at us while he was beating us. One time when one of my brothers was back from college, my dad beat him until he was down on the floor. Then he kicked him. I was scared to death.

"Along with the beatings, my dad forced us to go to church. I never learned of God's love there. We hated it. All of us turned the other way when we had the chance and ran just as fast as we could.

"There was also sexual abuse from my grandfather. I had to overcome the bitterness I felt towards my mother for not protecting us. She just stood back and turned her head or exited herself from the room.

"After graduating from high school, a friend asked me to come to California to live with her. When I told my parents good-bye, my dad told me I was never welcome back home and that he would never speak to me again.

"Taking the train, I stopped a couple of days in El Paso to visit Terry, a guy I used to date. When he picked me up at the train depot, I wasn't feeling well. I told him I needed to go to a motel, take some pain pills, get a hot bath, and rest. I would see him the next day.

"Terry took me to the motel and dropped me off. When I finished bathing, I walked into the other room and there was Terry sitting in a chair. Frightened, drugged, and sick, I was raped. He had signed into the motel as Mr. and Mrs. and had gotten a key from the desk clerk. I had nightmares about that for years.

"I got a job in California and my friend and I found a one-bedroom apartment. Working nights, she would arrive home about 1:00 in the morning and bring three or four guys with her. Dating a number of guys myself, I had such a poor self-concept that I really didn't care what happened to me. At the end of a year and a half, I was fed up and decided to go home. I thought my father would forgive me, but he told me I wasn't welcome.

"Bill, a former boyfriend, came home from Chicago and visited me while I was with my parents. He asked me to marry him even though we had only seen each other once in the past year and a half. I felt I didn't have much of a choice. I couldn't live with my folks, I didn't have enough money to go to school, and I didn't have a job.

"I married Bill and moved to Chicago, but it was not a good marriage. He was abusive, and in the first year and a half we separated three times.

"One day my mom called. My father was in the hospital in critical condition, and she wanted me to come and help. I was looking for a reason to go home, so I went. During this time my brother and his wife invited me to church in a town nearby. That morning I heard about the love of Jesus, and when the pastor gave an invitation to accept Christ as my personal Savior, I went forward to pray and ask Him into my life. I had never learned of God's love until that point. When Bill learned what had happened, he started coming to see me, and he also went forward to pray.

"After Dad came home from the hospital, I went back with Bill. By the end of the summer we were ready to divorce again. We moved back to Waterloo because the church was there, became involved in the church, started praying together, and he treated me well. It was the only normal part of our marriage.

"When things started going well, we decided to have children. I didn't get pregnant, so we decided to adopt. Our first adopted child, Kristin, was a preemie with a severe form of asthma. She was in the hospital four or five times that first year with dehydration.

"Because we couldn't live on Bill's salary, he found a job in a different town, and we moved. That was the end of our church attendance.

"When Kristin was eighteen months old, we got a call about adopting Tim. Because Kristin was frequently ill, I told Bill I was too exhausted to care for a second child, but he insisted, and we brought Tim home. Tim had frequent bronchitis and pneumonia, and now I had two sick children. I was also sick. When I went to see the doctor, I found out I was pregnant. Tim was sixteen months old when Adam was born.

"When Adam was two years old, Bill started beating him. One day Bill yelled at him and told him to quit eating like an animal. Adam got nervous and dropped spaghetti down the front of him. Bill kept yelling and cursing at him. Then he grabbed Adam's head, smashed it into his plate full of spaghetti, and rammed his face around in it. Picking up the edge of the table, he threw it over. The plates went flying through the air, and Bill went storming out of the house.

"The kids continued to be sick, and I got so run down that I was rushed to the hospital in a near coma. I dropped to ninety pounds, was continually nauseated and unable to sleep, had nightmares, and was unable to read and comprehend what I was reading. The left side of my body was completely numb, and I had migraines that lasted for days. Sometimes my brain went completely blank for minutes at a time. I ended up in the psychotherapy unit.

"When I was well enough to go home, Bill and I got in a fight one night and the next day he filed for divorce.

"Through counseling I learned to picture Christ with me in everything that had happened to me. Realizing He was always there to comfort me when I was hurting brought me comfort and healing. I learned to ask, 'What would Jesus do?' and live accordingly. I also prayed for my children that they would have healing of memories and grow up to be normal people.

"A beautiful illustration of Christ standing on the shore of a large sea really helped me. On the horizon a boat is coming toward Him. As it comes closer, one can see it has been in a horrible battle and is completely battle scarred. The mast is torn, the sails are ripped and tattered, and there are holes in everything. The boat represents me. Jesus is the Master Carpenter and is the only one who can restore the boat. As the boat reaches Him, He takes it, this life that I have been living, and begins to work. He repairs the holes, cleans the masts, washes and mends the sails, and clothes me in white. Now I am clean and whole again. As the boat leaves the shore, Jesus gets in and sails with me. Now I know He is always with me."

Today Jeanne is happily married to Bob, a wonderful Christian man. Instead of threatening, screaming, swearing, and throwing things, there is gentleness, love, caring, and understanding. God has used and is using Jeanne to reach many hurting people. She understands what they are feeling and willingly shares how God has helped her.

Jeanne adds, "The main verse I claimed when I was going through everything is in Lamentations 3:22-23 (KJ). 'It is of the Lord's mercies that we are not consumed, because His compassions fail not. They are new every morning: great is thy faithfulness.' "

My God Is Real

My God is real, I know He lives
No matter what men say.
It's something deep within my heart
That tells me it's this way.

For when my boat came in to shore
And needed much repair,
Jesus stood with outstretched arms
To love and mend me there.

He then did something no one else
Could even think to do.
He gave me purpose and a hope
And made my life anew.

There's nowhere else that man can find
Such joy and peace and love.
It's only God that makes it so.
He sends it from above.

So when you need that extra help
And need someone to care,
Remember He gives strength anew.
Your burdens He will bear.

Yes, God is real. I've found it so.
Just call on Him and see.
He's just as near as breath itself.
He's there for you and me.

Chapter 13

Dreary Days

I had been confined to our upstairs bedroom most of the month with a back problem. It had been raining all morning, and the boys were very restless. They desperately needed something to do, and I desperately needed something for them to do. When Kevin and Greg asked if they could go play ball with the neighborhood boys in the rain, I said "Yes." I made them promise, however, to play on the grass and stay out of the mud. Of course, they promised.

Kevin did manage to stay pretty clean, but Greg came in with mud from head to toe. Our washer and dryer were located in the upstairs bathroom, so we all managed to meet in there and get him cleaned up.

Walking out of the bathroom, I smelled smoke. Not being able to go downstairs, I sent the kids through the house to find the source of the smoke. When they couldn't find it, I went back to my bedroom. There to my great surprise were little wisps of smoke rising from my pillow which had fallen against the reading light attached to the headboard of my bed. The heat from the light had burned a fairly big hole in the pillow. I got back in bed thankful it had not started a fire.

Later that day, I could hear the downstairs phone ringing. Soon Sheryl came bounding up the stairs to inform me that the phone was no longer on the wall but was in the middle of the kitchen floor. I never did find out how it got there.

That evening Shelly and the children were getting ready to go to church. Just before they left, someone pulled the buffet drawer out too far, and it landed on the floor. This drawer was our "junk" drawer and held pencils, tacks, paper clips, erasers, and other miscellaneous items which were now scattered across the dining room floor. Before leaving to go to church, Shelly came up to kiss me good-bye and said, "Don't worry about a thing. When I get home, I'll get the scoop shovel and put it all back in the drawer."

As I lay alone in our big, quiet house, I felt totally discouraged. What a crazy day it had been. I felt useless both as a wife and as a mother. Did God really know what He was doing? None of it made any sense.

Finally, I prayed and told God how frustrated and useless I felt. As I prayed, a great transformation took place and I felt a great peace. God's presence was so real I felt I could reach out and touch Him. I wrote my feelings on a piece of paper and put the words to music. A few years later Lorenz Publishers bought and published my song, "The Presence of Jesus Surrounds Me."

The next few years I was in and out of the hospital and restricted many times to bed. The pain was no longer just in my back, but all over my body. I had severe aching, no energy, and many, many times it was difficult to do anything. During this time I visited in the home of some friends. Sitting on their porch one evening, I observed one of those gorgeous nights with a full moon and felt compelled to write a poem about it. When my friends read the poem, they encouraged me to write more poetry. I did, and those poems were later published in a book called, "There is Hope for Your World."

After many tests, the doctors found I have a problem that is not deteriorating but can often cause a lot of pain. With pain medication and much care not to overextend my limits, I can now keep it pretty well under control.

God has taught me many things through these experiences, but one of the most important is that God never wastes us. He set me aside for a little while to teach me more of Himself and to face me in a new direction. Through all of my tears and questioning, He was still there.

Sometimes it is in our worst times that we catch our best glimpses of God. Is there any greater experience than to see Jesus and to feel

His touch on our lives?

Luke 8:43-48 tells about a woman who had been subject to bleeding for twelve years. She was in a crowd and managed to get close enough to Jesus to touch the hem of His garment. Her bleeding stopped immediately. When Jesus asked who had touched Him, she knelt before Him and told Him what she had done. Jesus said to her, "Daughter, your faith has healed you. Go in peace."

What kind of peace does Jesus give? Philippians 4:7 describes it by saying, "You will experience God's peace, which is far more wonderful than the human mind can understand. His peace will keep your thoughts and your hearts quiet and at rest as you trust in Christ Jesus." (Liv)

Twelve years of bleeding brought this woman to Jesus. I wonder if she might have thought it was worth all of the suffering to receive a special touch from Him.

John 9:1-3 also tells about a man born blind. "As he (Jesus) went along, he saw a man blind from birth. His disciples asked him, 'Rabbi, who sinned, this man or his parents, that he was born blind?'

"'Neither this man nor his parents sinned,' said Jesus, 'but this happened so that the work of God might be displayed in his life.' "

Wow! As a result of this man's blindness, he not only met Jesus, but displayed His work. Verse 38 says, "The man said, 'Lord, I believe,' and he worshipped Him." If this man had not needed a miracle, he may never have found Jesus and received spiritual sight. I really believe that he would have said it was worth being blind for the privilege of seeing Jesus and finding eternal life.

Not only did those who were healed find Jesus, but many others who witnessed their healings also believed. What kind of a witness are we when we are in need of a special touch from God? He may or may not choose to heal us, but He may choose to use us. Are we willing to bring glory to Him through our suffering? We will have our dreary days, but God wants to bring us His peace and do a special work in us for His glory.

69

He Will See Me Through

When I have a heavy burden
I cannot bear alone,
Help me to know how much You love
And care for all Your own.

For I sometimes get discouraged
When Your way I cannot see,
And I may need reminded that
You have a plan for me.

Help me remember You're my strength,
On You I can rely.
That in Your presence there is peace,
And You will be close by.

Yes, You can work a miracle
When I can't do a thing,
If I will only trust You
And to You my burden bring.

So when those dreary days are here,
I know You'll see me through.
Your presence will be there to help.
You'll give me strength anew.

Chapter 14

Everything Lost

Jan & Larry's Story:

"It was awful!" Jan reflects. "The trucks came to haul stuff away, but the day they came for Larry's tractor did me in. He had so much pride in that tractor. We would all laugh when Dad would go out on it. He was in a different world. I stood and cried and cried and cried. I thought, 'They can't take his tractor!' But they did."

Jan and Larry were married between Larry's junior and senior year at college. Upon finishing school, Larry took a job teaching vocational agriculture. "I had a great desire to succeed financially," Larry shares. "First, we rented a house. Then we borrowed money, bought a lot, and built a house. We split the lot and built another house, sold the first house, and bought a farm. We moved, bought another farm, split off ten acres, built a house, and that's the way it went. Real estate was very good to us."

Enrolling their children in Bible School, Jan and Larry got involved in a good church. Jan says, "One day the pastor came over and presented the plan of salvation. We accepted Christ and started growing spiritually. Our marriage also improved a lot. In spite of our deep love for each other, it took the Lord to really put it together."

Larry shares, "We lost the last farm we bought. We were worth well over a half-million dollars on paper. A number of things contributed to that loss. We had formed a partnership with our oldest son Kirk. Just three months before, Kirk and I had renewed our borrowed money. They said we could borrow about whatever we wanted to borrow, so we were hitting it pretty hard. We were raising twenty-five hundred head of hogs. After refinancing, there was some disease in the hog herd and feed was high. Then Kirk came one day and said, 'Dad, I know that I have to leave the farm. The Lord is calling me into the pastorate.' I told him we would work it out. We would talk to the lender and we would buy him out. We did, and Jan and I assumed Kirk's debt.

"Less than two weeks after this we got a letter in the mail from the lender that said, 'Your loan has been reviewed and has been classified high risk. We're going to reappraise your real estate.' I went to meet with him. He said because Kirk was not in the operation anymore, and I didn't have the best health, we were considered high risk. They reappraised us, and in one sitting we lost a quarter of a million dollars of real estate appraisal. Then we got a letter that said our equity had gone from seventy-two percent to nineteen percent. The noose was around our neck, but I refused to believe we couldn't make it work. We tried everything. I finally realized we were powerless. I met with the lender and told him the farm was theirs.

"Meanwhile we had a seventy-five-thousand-dollar feed bill. Our attorneys advised us to file bankruptcy, but we wanted to be responsible. We moved back to town with only the shirts on our backs and with a huge feed bill."

Larry continues, "The day we met with our attorney, Jan asked about his family. His wife was ill, and Jan told him we would pray for her. That was the most peaceful meeting. We did not have any evil in our hearts, and we still don't."

Jan adds, "I had literally gotten down on my knees and prayed about that meeting. I begged the Lord to show me how to deal with it. During that meeting I could visualize Jesus hanging on the cross, suffering for us. I had total peace about it. When we walked out of there, we were able to shake their hands. It had to be the Lord.

"It was neat the way the Lord worked. The morning I would be down, Larry would encourage me, and the morning he would be down, the Lord would speak through me to encourage him. This happened time and time again."

Larry adds, "We didn't know where we were going to move, but we found a vacant house and moved in the next week. It was a beautiful home. We got it with a lease-purchase agreement, so we owned a new house. The Lord really blessed us.

"At that time we made a vow to the Lord that if there were any lessons of life that we could use to help other farm couples, we would do so. We knew there were hundreds of thousands of farmers experiencing the same thing we had experienced, and we wanted to find some way to help them. We became diversification specialists, taking inventory of human resources, land, labor, and machine equipment, and deciding what to do with it. That became the new hope. We went to California, viewed some operations, came back, and began the Rural Development Center at our local college.

"We saw a lot of hurting people, and we still meet new people daily. We started going out to different communities to speak, farmer to farmer. To this day it has helped more than three thousand farm families."

Jan adds, "Larry teaches international students at the Rural Development Center two days a week. He has students from Central America, South America, and Canada. He teaches them about diversification, and they're taking it home.

"We are in a partnership now. We have a cabin on the river bottom that we rent for church retreats and hunting groups. We also have the hunting preserve where people can hunt pheasant, quail, and partridge. This is licensed by the Department of Natural Resources. Then we have this place that triples as a bed and breakfast, a hunter's lodge, and our home."

Larry continues, "Each person who comes to hunt rather quickly gets the idea that we're doing business in different ways and for different reasons. When we have hunting parties to our home, Jan likes to fix the first evening meal. We give thanks before we eat, and they're conscious of pictures and things on our walls. We've had quite a few people write us back and comment that they didn't know there were clean, wholesome, Christian people still around in business."

Jan adds, "When they come to the house, they aren't allowed to smoke or drink alcohol. It's surprising how many people are glad we don't allow that. We're apprehensive with each group about feeding them right and treating them right. We pray about every group that comes.

"When people ask us to talk to them about what we've experienced and to pray with them and help them through their problems, we tell them it was prayer and the Lord that gave us strength."

When I asked Jan and Larry what helped them the most to get through those difficult times, they didn't hesitate with their answers.

Jan said "God made it clear to me that He was always there, and that He would never leave us. I think that was my greatest help."

Larry added, "When your feeling of self-worth, pride, and loss of earthly things are all overcoming you, you think of what Jesus went through. There is nothing that He doesn't understand."

Jan also talked about visualizing Jesus on the Cross and feeling his isolation. "That's given us a new relationship with Christ in feeling the hurt and wrong He's bearing for other people. We were praying for the people that were hurting us, and there is no bitterness and anger towards them."

As Kirk watched his parents suffer through the loss of their farm, it wasn't until much later that he learned the circumstances surrounding that loss. When he asked them why they had not told him, they answered, "If you had known, you may not have answered God's call to go into the ministry, and that was what really mattered." Today Kirk knows the joy of serving God full-time because his parents loved enough to give sacrificially.

For Jan and Larry all earthly possessions were lost, but as Larry says, "The Lord has put us in a situation that is much greater than what we had before."

Love

Love—one of the most powerful words
That man has ever known,
For love can turn the world around
When love is really shown.

It's like a salve upon a wound,
For healing it imparts.
From bitterness to peace and love,
It mends our broken hearts.

This love is not a human love
But sent from God above.
And it's only as we know Him
That we can share this love.

For love was manifested when
Christ died that we might live.
And as He freely gave to us,
We too should also give.

He prayed for those who did Him wrong
And loved them anyway.
With open arms He welcomed them
Although they'd gone astray.

So when you're tired and weary
And life may seem unfair,
If someone's wronged you, show them love
And also say a prayer.

Chapter 15

Finding Rest

My sister Bonnie is a farmer's wife and had just walked in from grinding feed for their cattle. She sat in an easy chair across from me in the living room. "The grinder just broke," she said.

It was 11:00 am. I looked at her, already weary from the chores of the day and glad to sit for a couple of minutes to rest.

"How do you cope?" I asked. "This spring you had a tornado wipe out your new cattle shed, killing three cows. This summer the drought took much of your crop, and what you did get was full of fungus. Your husband needs a major heart surgery, your best tractor is not running, your plow broke down in the field this weekend, and now your grinder is broken. Has anything else gone wrong?"

She looked at me and laughed. "I don't know," she answered. "I don't keep track."

"Seriously," I questioned. "How do you handle it?"

Her response was quick. "I believe I'm in God's will, for I pray for God's will in my life. Then I know that anything that does happen is okay with Him. If I know it's okay with Him, then it's okay with me. I also pray I will learn something from everything that happens to me, and that I'll learn what He wants me to learn. We are on this earth to get ready for heaven. If everything was all roses, we wouldn't grow at all. I too have asked, 'Why?' and said, 'I can't handle anymore!' but He promises not to give us any more than we can handle. Well, I have to get back to work," she said as she rose to leave. "There's still a lot to do."

Wow! I thought as I watched her go. *No wonder she copes so well. She has such an absolute trust and confidence in God that she really rests in Him.*

How do we find this kind of confidence and trust that enables us to rest in God?

First, forming a picture in our mind of who God is and how much He cares about us may help. If we totally trust someone, we have confidence in their integrity, their uprightness, and everything about them. Can I place my confidence in God's integrity, His uprightness, and everything about Him? I can if I believe God is who He says He is.

When I attended a ladies' retreat, the speaker had us do a verbal exercise by naming an attribute of God for each letter of the alphabet. By the time we went through the alphabet, we had a very revealing list of who God is. It is very encouraging to look at such a list and ask, "If this is my God, can He handle my problems?" My emphatic response is, "Yes!" and He will do so if we allow Him.

Secondly, we need to be convinced that God has the perfect plan for our life. We can then trust Him with that plan. Psalms 139:15-16 says, "My frame was not hidden from You when I was made in the secret place. When I was woven together in the depths of the earth, Your eyes saw my unformed body. All the days ordained for me were written in Your book before one of them came to be." What better planning could there be than this?

Thirdly, trust comes when we keep our focus on Jesus. Matthew 14:25-33 tells us why this is important. After a long, tiring day, the disciples were in a boat crossing the Sea of Galilee. The wind was strong, and their boat was being battered by the waves. Sometime between three and six in the morning they saw Jesus walking to them on the water. Thinking it was a ghost, they were frightened. Immediately, Jesus said to them, "Take courage! It is I. Don't be afraid."

How often have we felt we have reached the end of our ability to go on? We long for rest, but the storm rages on. Then we see Jesus! He comes to us saying, "Take courage! It is I. Don't be afraid." Do we watch for Him in the raging of our storm? Do we listen so we can hear His voice?

How relieved and excited the disciples must have felt when they realized it was Jesus they saw. Peter got out of the boat and started walking on the water to meet Him. He stayed on top of the water as long as he looked at Jesus, but when he saw the waves and heard the boisterous wind, he became afraid and began to sink. He cried, "Lord, save me!" Jesus reached out, took him by the hand, and lifted him up. His question to Peter was, "You of little faith. Why did you doubt?"

When our eyes are fixed on Jesus, no matter how bad the storm rages or how high the waves get around us, we can stay on top of things. It's when we take our eyes off Him and put them back on our circumstances that we become afraid and begin to sink. Then like Peter we cry, "Lord, save me," and Jesus reaches out His hand and lifts us up. His question to us is, "You of little faith. Why did you doubt?"

Fourthly, we need to develop and diligently pursue a close relationship with Christ. We need to pray for a hungering and thirsting after God so we can really get to know Him. The better we know His character, the easier it will be to trust Him.

We also learn to trust in God by experience. As we pray and find Him faithful in the little things, it becomes easier to trust Him in the bigger things. When our oldest son Kevin learned to drive the car, I was a good back seat driver. I wanted to make sure he stayed on the road. Gradually, however, experience taught me that he would do a good job. I learned to trust the driving to him and relax and enjoy the scenery. Sometimes I wonder if I will ever remember that Christ is faithful, and I need to trust the driving to Him. When I do, I can relax and enjoy the scenery.

Finally, Isaiah 50:7 says, "Because the Sovereign Lord helps me, I will not be disgraced. Therefore have I set my face like flint, and I know I will not be put to shame." Flint is hard. This is a mind set. I will determine that no matter what happens to me, I will trust God.

Shortly before Shelly lost his job a few years ago, he made the statement, "My security is not in my job. It is in God." The day he actually lost his job, we determined together to trust God for the days ahead. God was always faithful, and all of our needs were met.

I have a card on my refrigerator door that says, "God is God! Trust." One day Greg read the sign and asked what it meant. "That sign means," I explained, "that God is in charge of every circumstance in my life, and I am to trust Him with that circumstance regardless of what I see or how I feel about it."

As I write this, I realize I fall far short of totally trusting God in every circumstance. I hope, however, that each of us will learn more and more to trust Him until we too can leave it up to Him to do whatever or allow whatever in our lives. It is only when we do this that we can find real rest in Him.

Keep Your Eyes Above

The Bible says that Peter walked
On water one dark night.
He walked to Jesus until wind
And waves filled him with fright.

He suddenly began to sink.
"Lord, save me!" he cried out.
Immediately Christ took his hand.
He asked, "Why did you doubt?"

Now circumstances didn't change,
But Peter's outlook did;
For when He started watching waves,
His view of Christ was hid.

So always keep your eyes above
And not on things you fear.
Then you'll find strength to walk through storms
Of life that you find here.

And as you put your trust in Him,
He'll give sweet rest to you.
For He is God and cannot fail,
And what He says He'll do.

Chapter 16

Daffodils

Prudence's Story:

"My mother loved the scriptures and read Bible stories to me every day," shares Prudence. "My Dad also had family devotions every morning; consequently, I learned scripture very young.

"When I was six, we had an evangelist visiting in our home. He spoke about a king who ate grass, and I said, 'That was Nebuchadnezzar.'

"'Amazing, he exclaimed, 'She can pronounce Nebuchadnezzar perfectly!'

"'That's not all,' I said. 'I can spell it,' and I spelled Nebuchadnezzar.

"When I graduated from high school, the lady fitting me with my cap and gown found a lump under my arm. A few years later I noticed a swelling in that lump, and the doctors found it was cancerous. They did surgery, and it was very successful.

"Fourteen years after my first experience with cancer, I had a different type of cancer. Another operation was performed to remove that tumor.

"Four years after that, I was stepping out of the car one day when I felt something crunch in my back, and I went to the ground. For the next three months I lay in the hospital, experiencing back pain and undergoing therapy.

When released, continued therapy didn't help. I had to sleep on the couch at home because I couldn't climb the steps to get to my bedroom. I mostly catnapped. Working at a bank, I was exhausted and unproductive. I would stand in the corner of a restroom stall, bracing my feet so I could rest. I would fall asleep standing up for a few minutes and then go back to my desk. By this time I had pain running down my right leg which was numb. I would work a few hours and go home.

"Back at Rochester, they discovered more cancer, and surgery was performed on my right ankle and a plastic piece inserted that facilitated walking. I did not walk alone for eight months, and I got very little sleep. Lying on the floor while putting my legs and feet on the sofa seemed to be my only relief from the pain.

"After the surgery, a Realtor friend who had asked me numerous times to come and work with him came and asked me again. Knowing I was not the type of person who could lie around in pain and do nothing, I decided real estate might be the answer for me until the Lord called me home.

"While talking on the phone upstairs one Friday, the doorbell rang. Not taking time to put on my leg brace to come down the steps, I came down four steps and hit the landing, my leg buckling under me. I went down the rest of the way on my back. I was barely able to get up and answer the door. The x-ray on Monday showed a broken pelvis in three places. I had been walking around on it for three days! Back to the hospital I went.

"A pelvis can't be set. For three months I lay waiting for it to heal. It was terrible. There were bed sores on my left hip and my left elbow. We finally put rubber cushions on them so they would do better.

"Two years ago, I woke up one night with a lot of pain in my eye. When I got up the next morning, I realized I couldn't see out of that eye. Through an ophthalmologist I learned the main blood vessel supplying blood to the eye had detached and hemorrhaged. The doctor said there was a possibility that the other eye might do the same thing. It could happen in three weeks or in several years. Every day I have so much to give thanks for because I can still see out of my right eye.

"My last operation was last summer. I woke up during the night and my right thumb hurt so bad I didn't know what to do. It continued to get worse until I couldn't use it. The doctors found a tumor on the tendon that controls the thumb. Surgery was done and my hand was placed in a brace type of cast which I wore for five months. I started chemotherapy again.

"I have pain all of the time. It's a rare, rare time when I awake feeling refreshed and rested. I usually get up several times a night because I just can't lie there anymore. I have had one hundred seventeen chemotherapy treatments so far. When they found cancer in my spine a number of years ago, they only gave me four years to live. I have lived ten years beyond what they said.

"I sometimes think the Lord allowed my illness so I would go into real estate and be a better witness for Him. When I show houses to new customers, I give them a scripture text as a housewarming gift. I also try to take them out for coffee or refreshments as quickly as I can with the express purpose of ministering. I start by giving thanks for the food. That immediately opens up avenues to talk about the Lord.

"Ever since I got sick I have felt that time is of the essence. Every day counts! I have this insatiable thirst to memorize more scripture, especially since there is a possibility I could lose the sight in my other eye.

"I carry a great burden for the salvation of people. Time is so short, not just for me but for everyone. Sometimes I think that's why I'm not able to sleep at night; not just because I have pain, but I have a pain in my heart that there are so many people that I should be witnessing to, and I haven't been able to do it. I want to use every minute as wisely as I can.

"I have worked with the cancer society for the past twenty years. They have a special day called Daffodil Day. Last year I gave daffodils to the local hospital. I wrapped them up with a tract inside along with my name. This year I gave them to the people who get Meals on Wheels. As a result, an elderly gentlemen called and said he had accepted the Lord.

"Psalms 37-40 are very precious chapters to me. I once read those scriptures to Don, my fiancé, when he was in the hospital. He was in a large ward, and there were probably seventy or eighty people there. Everything came to a halt, and they listened.

"It's interesting. The Lord has kept me healthy enough to be able to work, sick enough to know I'm not doing it by myself, and dependent enough upon Him to know He is the one taking care of the situation."

May Others See Jesus in Me

I've suffered much while here on earth
And yet miraculously,
I see God's love and know He has
A special plan for me.

A plan I may not understand,
But that's okay, you see.
For I know the One who holds my hand,
And that's enough for me.

I feel His gifts of love to me
In spite of pain I feel.
Gifts I want to share and so
I pray now as I kneel.

Give me a vision for lost souls
And somehow, Lord, use me.
That through my suffering You will shine,
And Jesus Christ they'll see.

Please show me how to reach them,
That I may let them know
That You are real, alive today,
And that You love them so.

That You can give them happiness,
Real joy and peace of mind.
For we are empty without God
And peace we cannot find.

So help me, Lord, to show Your love
In everything I do,
That others will see Christ in me
And they will know You, too.

Chapter 17

Are We Listening?

A friend once related how her daughter and friend tried to make waffles for the first time. They plugged in the waffle iron and poured in some batter without preheating the iron. Thinking that when the light shut off their waffle would be ready, they lifted the lid. Batter ran everywhere!

Deciding they should have greased the waffle iron first, they tried again. This time they waited for the light to come on before taking their waffle out. When they lifted the lid, half of the waffle was stuck on the top of the iron, half was stuck on the bottom, and the middle was runny and doughy.

I laughed as I visualized the two girls trying to make their waffles. The only thing that kept them from having delicious, perfect waffles was their lack of instruction. Preheating the waffle iron would have made all of the difference.

We need to know what God's instructions are for us by spending time with Him in Bible reading, prayer, and fellowship. As we do so, we will find the strength we need to go through our trials. David writes in Psalms 16:8, "I have set the Lord always before me. Because He is at my right hand, I will not be shaken."

The Bible is God's Word to us. 2 Timothy 3:16 says, "All scripture is God-breathed and is useful for teaching, rebuking, correcting, and training in righteousness." If we are to know God's character, we must read His Word.

We also need to spend time in prayer. As we pray, we communicate with our Heavenly Father. It is a time of thanksgiving, intercession, and petitioning. Someone once said, "Prayer is not an option. It is a necessity!"

If we feel discouraged because we don't feel we know how to pray, Romans 8:26 says, "In the same way, the Spirit helps us in our weakness. We do not know what we ought to pray for, but the Spirit Himself intercedes for us with groans that words cannot express."

I am impressed with the amount of time Jesus spent in prayer. Luke 5:16 tells us, "But Jesus often withdrew to lonely places and prayed." Luke 6:12 says, "One of those days Jesus went out to a mountainside to pray, and spent the night praying to God." If Jesus spent this much time in prayer, surely we should pray.

Fellowship with God is also important. I remember my two-year-old granddaughter Maria coming to me one day. Her little face was turned up to mine, her dark eyes full of excitement. She clutched her story book tightly against her chest as she reached out her free hand to take hold of mine. "C'mon, Gama, c'mon!" she begged.

I was busy, but how could I refuse? My job would keep. If I let this moment pass, it would be gone forever. We settled comfortably in the rocking chair, and I read *The Three Little Pigs* with all the fervor I could muster.

" 'Little pig, little pig, let me come in,' said the wolf.

" 'No, No, not by the hair of my chinny chin, chin,' answered the little pig."

"No! No!" declared Maria, as she shook her finger at the big bad wolf.

I thought about this precious little life snuggled close to me and realized that sometimes I just need to cuddle up close to my Heavenly Father with all of the trust and confidence in Him that Maria had in me. Can I say, "Lord, Jesus, I just want to enjoy this time together, forgetting about the cares of this world to spend some treasured moments with you?"

Probably the hardest thing to do in spending time with God is to be quiet and listen to what He has to say to us. One evening Shelly and I were watching the halftime entertainment of the Orange Bowl on television. The crowds were cheering, singers were singing, laser beams were flashing, the band was playing, and hundreds of balloons were being released. There was noise, noise, noise!

What a sharp contrast to the quiet mentioned in Psalm 23:2-3a! "He makes me lie down in green pastures, He leads me beside quiet waters, He restores my soul..."

The Lord said to Elijah in 1 Kings 19:11-12, "Go out and stand on the mountain in the presence of the Lord, for the Lord is about to pass by. Then a great and powerful wind tore the mountains apart and shattered the rocks before the Lord, but the Lord was not in the wind. After the wind there was an earthquake, but the Lord was not in the earthquake. After the earthquake came a fire, but the Lord was not in the fire. And after the fire came a *gentle whisper.*"

We may often want to look for God in the great and spectacular—in a great and powerful wind, an earthquake, or a fire, but God's voice comes in a gentle whisper. Psalm 46:10 says, "Be still, and know that I am God."

God needs to be number one in our life. Standing in my kitchen getting supper one day, I heard our car drive into the garage and I knew Shelly was home. Hardly noticing me, he hurried to the television set explaining with great excitement that the Hawkeyes were playing and "wonder of wonders they were ahead!" In a few minutes it was halftime and he came back to the kitchen. Giving me a hug and a kiss, he grinned and said, "You're important, too."

I could laugh with him because I never have to question whether I am important to him. He shows me in many different ways. I know I'm the Number One person in his life.

Can God tell that He is Number One in our lives? Are we listening to His voice to hear what He wants to say to us? In a busy world, finding time to spend with God may be hard to do, but it is essential for a victorious walk with Him. May we be diligent in guarding our time alone with Him.

Wait Awhile With Quiet Heart

We sometimes are impatient.
We just don't like to wait.
We think we have to have things now,
And we don't hesitate.

We hurry here, we hurry there
With lots of animation.
Our pace just never seems to slow
With jets and aviation.

We speed along so fast sometimes
Our world we just don't see.
We've instant coffee, instant meals
And instant aids and tea.

But we need some time to listen,
To take a look around,
That we may see God's beauty
And blessings that abound.

Take time to hear the birds that sing,
To watch the raindrops fall,
To smell the lilacs as they bloom
And hold the babe so small.

We also need to take some time
To simply sit and wait,
To have some quiet time with God,
To pray and meditate.

Then we will find that down through life
When trials come our way,
We'll always find the strength we need
To make it through the day.

Chapter 18

One Special Lady

Darlene's Story:

I got acquainted with Darlene through my sister-in-law Karen. She would say, "Darlene is one special lady. You have got to meet her!" When I finally did, I knew that Karen was right. She is one special lady.

"Leon was a farmer, and we married as soon as I graduated from high school." Darlene relates, "We looked like a perfect storybook family. Leon was musical and successful, and he built me a gorgeous brick house. We had three intelligent, wonderful children, Sandra, Kim, and Brian, who were also musical. I should have been in my glory, but I never was. I knew there had to be more to life. I became more and more faithful to the church, searching for something to fill the emptiness I felt.

"One evening Billy Graham came on the television, and I sat spellbound in front of the set. With tears running down my face, I knelt and prayed the prayer of repentance. I was overwhelmed with the transformation I felt. I saw everything so differently. Looking at my family, I realized for the first time that we had everything but were so lost we had nothing.

"When Sandra was a senior in high school, I was diagnosed with Hodgkin's disease. A large tumor had grown in my lung area on the left side. When surgery was done with the intent to take out the lung and the tumor, they found the tumor was in the lymph system and could not be removed, so they gave me radiation treatments. Ten days later they did another surgery to remove the spleen to do a biopsy of all the lymph nodes in my abdominal area and to check the liver.

"The radiation treatments made me very ill. I lost all of my hair, weighed about eighty-two pounds, and was tube fed. Shortly after going home from the hospital, a pastor prayed for my healing. He made it clear that God is the one who heals, but that He doesn't always choose to heal. When He does heal, there's a reason. He also said that I must follow my doctor's orders. I had an overwhelming peace, and I knew that God had healed me of cancer.

"The next day I had an x-ray, and the doctor said I had a new growth behind the original growth in my lungs. Two days later I had three doctors at Mayo Clinic tell me that because of the size of this tumor, I would not live three months. I needed to have it surgically removed. I said, 'No!', that I was going home for Thanksgiving and Christmas and would see them later. Miraculously, at the end of three months, all signs of cancer were gone. God had healed me. We sang praises to God all the way home.

"A few years ago my husband, who was a strong, healthy man, had a massive stroke. He became totally blind and totally dependent. After four months of rehabilitation and hospitalization, the doctor advised that we should take him to the head injury foundation in Denver. When we arrived, I learned a Billy Graham Crusade was in town. Convinced I needed to take Leon, I got the doctor's consent. It took two orderlies and unbelievable preparation to get him there, but God worked it out. Leon's idols, Johnny Cash and Jean Carter, were the guests. After hearing Johnny Cash sing and give his testimony and Billy Graham preach, Leon asked to go forward. They wheeled his wheelchair forward and prayed with him, and his spirit was reached.

"During Leon's hospitalization, Brian ran the farm operation, and I trained in nursing skills. Eight months after the stroke, we were able to bring Leon home.

"Nine months after Leon came home, the Lord took Brian home to be with Him. He had picked up a pipe to shake out some dirt.

There was a heavy-duty high-line wire above the pipe that went into the motor of the irrigation well. The pipe never came in contact with the wire, but because the current was so strong, and because Brian was standing in water holding the pipe, the current went through the metal and through Brian's body. When I got to him, he was lying in the field. I gave him CPR, but there was no response. Brian had accepted the Lord in college, so I knew he was ready to go. I said to him, 'Brian, Dad and I will be okay. You can go home to be with the Lord. The Lord will take care of us.' I knew the moment he physically was no longer with me. There was such a sense of peace. If Brian heard me or not, only God knows, but I felt that Brian heard me tell him good-bye.

"With Leon totally dependent on others, and with Brian gone, I had a great fear, for I had never been without a male figure in my life. God gave me comfort with Isaiah 54:5. 'For your Maker is your husband, the Lord Almighty is His name, the Holy One of Israel is your Redeemer; He is called the God of all the earth.' I had to go directly to the Lord and see Him as my husband, and He has taken care of me in every way. He's always there.

"When I could no longer take care of Leon and had to put him in a health care facility, he used to cry out for me hourly. I couldn't run fifty miles every time he called, so I had to learn to give him to God. 2 Chronicles 20:15 says, 'Do not be afraid or discouraged....For the battle is not yours, but God's.' I claimed that verse daily for Leon. God could give him the same peace that He had given me.

"Sometimes Leon's body would move, and his legs would get very spastic. He would cry out in anxiety. It was unbearable for me to see him like this. The only thing they could do for him was to give him drugs. These would deaden the brain, but the spasms would continue. One day when he was in this condition, I started reading scripture to him. Gradually he became less spastic and very peaceful. Now those who take care of Leon know the only thing that helps him during his highly spastic times is the Word of God. As a result of this, others have committed their lives to Christ.

"Sometimes I find it's hard to know how to pray for Leon. He may know you or he may not. I have prayed for his complete healing, and I have prayed for God to take him home. Now I just pray for peace for his day and that God will use this situation however He chooses. The Lord still ministers through Leon even in the condition he is in. Many have shared how he has encouraged them and said the things they needed to hear.

"I really love Romans 12:1-2 (Liv): 'I plead with you to give your bodies to God. Let them be a living sacrifice, holy - the kind He can accept. When you think of what He has done for you, is this too much to ask? Don't copy the behavior and customs of this world, but be a new and different person with a fresh newness in all you do and think. Then you will learn from your own experience how His ways will really satisfy you.'

"The grace and love of God I have experienced in these times have been far beyond any of the suffering and trauma I have gone through. I wouldn't change any part of my suffering because I would never have experienced God's grace the way I have. I can go to the Word, rely on the Lord, and trust. God is so full of grace and so faithful that sometimes I become overwhelmed by His goodness!"

Thank You for Loving Me

My heart is filled with gratitude
For all Your love and care,
For all the miracles of life
And ways you answer prayer.

I thank You for the answers
To prayers I can't yet see,
For You have promised You will hear,
And You will answer me.

You're there when I have problems,
You're there when I have doubts;
Or when I question life and say,
"What is it all about?"

And if I wonder and ask why,
Please take me by the hand
And I will know that all is well
As in Your strength I stand.

For I will know You know all things
Whatever they may be,
And I will trust You even though
The answers I can't see.

So thank You for Your loving care,
For miracles I see,
For always being by my side,
Thank You for loving me!

Chapter 19

Sand

When Kevin was three, he was playing in some sand with a friend. We weren't paying very much attention to them, but we knew they were having a good time carrying their little buckets of sand around. Shelly, who worked second shift, usually rode his motorcycle to work. When it was time to leave, he noticed sand around the gas cap and a neat little pile of sand on the ground below his motorcycle. Taking the gas cap off and looking inside, he saw a gas tank full of sand. Although the truth was obvious, he found the boys and asked if they had put sand in the gas tank. Their very serious response was, "No, just gas!"

Sometimes we may unintentionally put "sand" into someone's life by a harsh word, a sarcastic remark, or a judgmental attitude. Little grains of sand may seem harmless enough, but they may do a lot of damage.

How do we comfort those who are suffering without putting "sand" in their lives? Sometimes it is difficult to know how to comfort the one who is hurting. Everything we say seems to be so inadequate to express our love and concern and to bring them the comfort they need. We may, therefore, stay away, rationalizing that they will be better off without us.

Sometimes we may not need to say much of anything. We may just need to be there with a hug and our presence. When we lost our son-in-law in a fire, an elderly couple came one evening and brought donuts. They didn't say much, but we sat around the table, ate our donuts, and prayed together. I have always remembered their kindness in just being there to let us know they cared. People usually aren't looking for explanations or profound revelations. They just need to know we care. It's much better to say too little than too much.

A hurting friend surprised me one day by saying, "I thought if one more person quoted Romans 8:28 to me, I would just die!" I thought about this verse: "And we know that in all things God works for the good of those who love Him, who have been called according to His purpose." This verse has been an encouragement and comfort to me in some of my most difficult times, and her statement left me perplexed. If I have verses that have helped me, shouldn't I share them with others?

My question was answered by the example of another friend. She cautiously approached me one day with a verse she had in mind for me. She said, "Now, I have a verse that has really helped me. If you want to hear it, I will be glad to share it with you. If you don't, that's quite alright."

I wanted to hear the verse. It was, in fact, so relevant to my situation that I memorized it, and it has encouraged me many times since. I was very glad my friend had shared her verse with me.

The way we share with others may make all of the difference in the way it is received. My friend approached me with such love and concern that I knew she really cared. If she had approached me with a smile and a pat on my back and said, "Now you know everything is going to work out just fine! Remember Romans 8:28!" my response would have been much different.

2 Corinthians 1:3-4 tells us to comfort with the same comfort we have received from God. "Praise be to the God and Father of our Lord Jesus Christ, the Father of compassion and the God of all comfort, who comforts us in all our troubles, so that we can comfort those in any trouble with the comfort we ourselves have received from God." How does God comfort? With understanding, forgiveness, kindness, love, and mercy.

We have an Indian prayer hanging in our kitchen that says, "Grant that I may not criticize my neighbor until I have walked a mile in his moccasins." When we want to give quick answers to someone, we can remember that we may not know all of the circumstances involved. We too need to respond with understanding, forgiveness, kindness, love, and mercy. Only God knows for sure about the little grains of sand in their moccasins.

Seeds of Comfort

I see the seeds as they come down
From great, tall trees around,
Some floating in soft cotton balls,
Some spinning to the ground.

The seeds are blown beyond the trees
To places yet unknown
Where some will land to root and sprout
And someday be full grown.

What kind of seeds do I send out
In things I do and say?
For they will go, I know not where,
To sprout and grow someday.

Will they be seeds to help someone,
To brighten someone's day?
Or be as dandelion seeds
That cause so much dismay?

So I pray this prayer to You, Oh Lord,
"Help me along life's way,
That I will never have regrets
For things I do or say.

May I never be judgmental
Or harsh to those around,
But may I always speak in love
That Your love may abound.

Help me to show much patience,
Be sensitive to needs,
And may I comfort others, Lord
In loving words and deeds.

And when I sometimes make mistakes,
Forgive me, this I pray,
For with Your help I'll show Your love
The best I can each day.

Yes, help me be a blessing
In seeds I spread about,
And any seed that's not from you,
I pray will never sprout.

Chapter 20

Paralyzed!

Shirley's Story:

"It was spring break, and my husband George, our five-year-old daughter, Alisha, and I had been to visit my sister and her husband," Shirley shares. "Heading home that morning, we hit a slippery spot on the road. The car swerved, caught gravel, and we went flying through the air. Flipping over, it landed upside down on its hood. While still in mid-air, George and I both shouted simultaneously, 'Lord, help us!'

"After we landed, George asked if I could move. I couldn't. I had heard my neck crack, and I was sure it was broken. As George skillfully managed to get me out through the popped out windshield, I opened my eyes. It was then that I knew what I was guessing was true. I was paralyzed! In my memory I was still in a sitting position, but now as I looked, I knew it was me only by seeing my own legs trailing behind me. Alisha was not hurt except for a cut on her eyelid and a cut on her hand that needed stitches.

"Lying there waiting for the ambulance, I thought about Psalm 112:7 in the Living Bible. 'He does not fear bad news, nor live in dread of what may happen. For he has settled in his mind that Jehovah will take care of him.' I meditated on that verse and thought about all of the things I had been taught through the years about giving thanks and praying.

"My Christian walk had started years before as a sophomore in college. There I heard that faith in just anything is not good enough, for a person can be very sincere and still be very wrong. One must follow Jesus Christ. That's the first time I saw a clear difference between living a moral life that adhered to Christian beliefs and really making a commitment to Christ. Proverbs 14:12 says, 'There is a way that seems right to a man, but in the end it leads to death.' Going back to my room, I prayed, 'Dear, Lord, I am tired of trying to live both sides of the fence. I just want to be on Your side.' From that time on my interest in the Lord and the Word of God really sparked.

"During my senior year of college, I was challenged with John 15:5. 'I am the vine; you are the branches. If a man remains in Me and I in him, he will bear much fruit; apart from Me you can do nothing.' That verse had a great influence on my life because it opened up to me the vital relationship we can have with the Lord.

"Following the accident, I was in hospitals for a year. To help pass the time, I would think of as many Bible verses as I could until I couldn't think anymore. It was very hard to concentrate with all of the pain, but it was a real comfort to me.

"Without full use of my legs and arms, I am a quadriplegic. It was hard to begin to hear people call me that, especially that first day. I was at the mercy of everyone. Sometimes I might cough and need a tissue, and nobody was there to help, or my nose would be running, and no one was there to wipe it. I might raise my arm above my head and not be able to get it back down. Because I couldn't grasp or reach for things, I had to have a special kind of buzzer to call a nurse on the calling system. Sometimes I could only use my very weak voice and hope someone would hear me. When someone finally came, I would sometimes get bawled out because I had interrupted what they were doing.

"One nurse was particularly ungracious and irritable. I tried very hard to be sympathetic to her by being understanding of her needs and showing my concern for her.

"I had another nurse, however, who was a wonderful Christian and a very cheerful person. We had many good times together. She would say to me, 'Now remember, when you are in therapy and things are hard, you have a power in you that many other people don't have.' Then she would quote scripture verses about the power that raised Christ from the dead and look at me very intently while she shared these things. She would remind me very firmly that this was true and worthy of remembering!

"My daughter Alisha has been a real joy and encouragement to me. My sister used to tell her that her cheerful smile was one of my bottles of medicine. There are so many things I would like to be able to do with her, but I can't. Someone else has to take us shopping, and others taught her how to cook, sew, and develop skills. We thank the Lord for all of these people.

"I am also very thankful for my kind, gentle husband George. He could have just walked away from the situation, but when we were married, he made a commitment both to me and the Lord, and it was never an issue.

"We did have some very frustrating times, however. Besides having many new responsibilities, such as figuring taxes, George had to learn how to take care of me. Sometimes we were at each other and had to be reminded who the enemy was. Life is much more enjoyable for us now than it was a few years ago.

"George did a lot of work on the house to get it ready for me. He remodeled the rooms, enlarging them and making them accessible to my wheelchair. He also invented things for me. One of the best things he invented was my bed. When I came home from the hospital, he had to get up every two hours to turn me so I wouldn't get bed sores. Now he has two air mattresses rolled up with a timer on them. One inflates and puts me partly on one side, and then it gradually lifts so it doesn't wake me up and goes to the other side.

"I have learned to use a computer and an electric typewriter by holding a pencil stick on my fingers with a piece of velcro. I'm also teaching music and Bible in a Christian school. A friend said to me, 'God's purpose doesn't end when something difficult like this happens. He continues using us in whatever way He has chosen.' It's encouraging to know God can still use me.

"I have never doubted God's existence in all of this. That question was settled long before the accident. Sometimes I did struggle, however, with why God allowed me to experience such an accident. He reminded me that others have suffered similarly. I also dealt with guilt feelings, thinking that perhaps if my attitudes had been better, maybe this wouldn't have happened. My pastor often said to me, 'God was not asleep when this happened. He was in control during all of that time.'

"A number of people have told me they know it is God's will for me to be healed. Sometimes I have felt like I owed them an apology for not getting healed. Others have said that if you say it enough times, it will happen. I finally decided that God was going to do what He was going to do regardless of what I thought. Now I just rest in the fact that God is in control, and He has the power to heal if He chooses.

"We try to live one day at a time just resting in the Lord. He meets us when we need Him as we need Him. We thank and praise Him!"

Trust in the Lord

(Proverbs 3:5-6)

"Trust in the Lord" is our command,
Now that sounds easy to do.
When things go right, it's easy to trust,
But when things go wrong, trust Him, too.

Now the rest of the verse says, "With all of your heart,"
That means through the good and the bad.
We don't need to question or even ask why.
Just trust Him and you will be glad.

"Lean not on your own understanding,"
We try to figure things out.
But God in His wisdom knows far more than we.
Only He knows what it's about.

"In all of your ways acknowledge Him."
Give Him first place in your life.
Trust Him to know what is best for you,
Whether in peace or in strife.

"And He shall direct your path."
What a comfort to be in His care.
Stay close to Him and He'll guide you aright.
Every trial He'll help you to bear.

Chapter 21

Never Say "Never!"

"I will never forgive that person as long as I live!" I heard my friend say. I couldn't believe what I was hearing. Thirty years earlier someone had done something to upset her, and she was still holding a grudge. The incident seemed so insignificant to me that I couldn't imagine why it mattered then, let alone now.

Jesus had some pretty powerful words to say concerning forgiveness. Matthew 6:12 (Liv) says, "And forgive us our sins, *just as we have forgiven* those who have sinned against us."

This is a pretty sobering thought, for there are no options here. If I want God to forgive me according to the standards I forgive, I had better make sure I forgive.

Jesus continues in verses 14-15. "Your heavenly Father will forgive you *if* you forgive those who sin against you; *but if you refuse to forgive them, He will not forgive you.*" Wow! Pretty scary!

I cannot emphasize enough how important it is for us to forgive. It is not something we do only when we feel like it; it is something we do in obedience to God. I am convinced that one of the most effective weapons Satan uses to bring disunity among God's people is an unforgiving spirit.

Receiving a long, hateful letter in the mail one day, I sat down immediately to write this person back and defend my position. I was hurt, and I was upset by the accusations that were made. As I started to write, however, the Holy Spirit brought conviction to my heart. I knew I had to forgive that person and respond in love. Although at that moment it seemed like an impossible task, in obedience to God

I wrote a different kind of a letter, one I felt was pleasing to Him. It wasn't until after I mailed the letter that God brought peace to my heart and did what I could not do. He took the frustration and animosity away, replaced it with His love, and allowed me to see a soul that needed God.

A young man nineteen years of age shared the following story with me. "When I was seventeen, I dated this girl. One day I was walking in the mall with another girl when the first girl saw me. It must have made her very jealous and angry because the next thing I know, she charged me with three counts of sexual battery and rape. When taken to court and convicted, I did community service and was put on probation. It was a real blow to me.

"Through this experience I was humbled beyond belief. I had always loved school, but I took so much slander from the kids, I hated to go anymore. They called me rapist and all sorts of things. Any self-worth I had, it took away. It was the worst thing that ever happened to me.

"As I prayed and gave this situation to God, He gave me Psalm 31:9-13. 'Be merciful to me, Oh Lord, for I am in distress; my eyes grow weak with sorrow, my soul and my body with grief. My life is consumed by anguish and my years by groaning; my strength fails because of my affliction, and my bones grow weak. Because of all my enemies, I am the utter contempt of my neighbors; I am a dread to my friends—those who see me on the street flee from me. I am forgotten by them as though I were dead; I have become like broken pottery. For I hear the slander of many; there is terror on every side; they conspire against me and plot to take my life.'

"That's what my life was like after being accused of rape. I found comfort, however, in the verses that followed. 'But I trust in you, Oh Lord; I say, You are my God. My times are in your hands; deliver me from my enemies and from those who pursue me. Let your face shine on your servant; save me in your unfailing love. Let me not be put to shame, Oh Lord, for I have cried out to You; but let the wicked be put to shame and lie silent in the grave. Let their lying lips be silenced, for with pride and contempt they speak arrogantly against the righteous.'

"The main thing that I struggled with was forgiving the girl. I'm not allowed to speak to her because of a court order, but someday I know the Lord will bring her back to me so I can say to her face, 'I forgive you.'

"I no longer have a burden. Since I gave it to the Lord, it has all been lifted. The exciting thing is that He has taken this tragedy in my life and turned it around for good. Because of what happened, I have been able to share Christ with people who are going through similar problems, and two of them have accepted the Lord."

This is a beautiful story! This young man learned an important lesson in forgiveness at a very young age. By the standards of the world, he would have had every right to be resentful and bitter, but because he chose to forgive, God has lifted his burden and is using him to reach others for Christ.

1 Peter 4:8 says, "Above all, love each other deeply, because love covers over a multitude of sins." Love is an important ingredient in the recipe of forgiveness. The more we love someone, the easier it is to forgive them.

It is impossible in ourselves to love everyone. Sometimes it is a choice in just being obedient to God. As we allow God's love to dwell in us, however, His love fills us and flows out to love others through us. As this happens, we can forgive others with the same forgiveness that God has forgiven us. If I really love someone, how can I not forgive him, or, if I haven't forgiven him, how can I say I really love him?

What kinds of hurts are we hanging on to and allowing to fester within us? What are those grudges we are holding that we need to forgive? Can we pray with the Psalmist in Psalms 139:23-24, (KJ): "Search me, O God, and know my heart: try me, and know my thoughts: And see if there be any wicked way in me, and lead me in the way everlasting."

Can we ask God to keep our hearts open so that nothing will hinder the work that He wants us to do and so that nothing will cloud the reality of Jesus Christ in our lives? We cannot be filled with anger, resentment, or hatred if we want to be effective for Christ. As one drop of ink pollutes the whole jar of water, so the sin of unforgiveness pollutes our lives. Never say, "I will never forgive!"

Help Me to Forgive

(1 Corinthians 13)

My heavenly Father will forgive
If I forgive men, too.
But only as His love indwells
Can I forgive, it's true.

His love is patient, always kind,
And it will never boast.
It is not jealous, neither proud,
But thinks of others most.

Love isn't rude nor wants its way.
For right and truth it longs.
It never angers easily
Nor keeps a score of wrongs.

For evil it has no delight.
It's glad when truth wins out.
It always trusts and ever hopes
And spreads goodwill about.

Yes, love is loyal, ever true.
It always thinks the best.
It will not fail but persevere,
Stand true in every test.

So when I feel that I've been wronged,
Please show me how to live.
Then put Your love within my heart
And help me to forgive.

A love that covers every wrong
And also sets me free.
For if I love and I forgive,
Then I'll have victory.

Chapter 22

Walking By Faith

Carol's Story:

"It was while I was attending college that I decided no matter what the cost, I was going to follow the Lord," Carol shares. "Jim Elliot, a martyred missionary, said, 'He is no fool who gives what he cannot keep to gain what he cannot lose.' That quote really impressed me, and I decided there really wasn't anything else for which I wanted to give my life.

"Between my sophomore and junior year of college, I went to a Navigator conference and met Keith. The next summer we were also there, and Keith became convinced that I was the girl that God had for him. He wrote and we got together, but I just didn't have any response, so we dropped it.

"Before Keith went to the mission field, God gave him a verse that said, 'Prepare your work in the field without, and afterward build your house.' He said, 'Okay, Lord. I'll go.' After a year, he wrote me a letter and proposed.

"Marrying Keith would mean that I was marrying someone I didn't really know, marrying a doctor, and marrying someone who felt he would be on the mission field the rest of his life. As I prayed about it, however, I felt that God was in it. When I said, 'Yes,' God very definitely put a love in my heart for Keith and a desire to be in Nigeria. In each situation since then we have always said, 'Lord, if Your presence doesn't go with us, don't take us.' Keith waited seven years from the time we met until we married.

"Mark 8:34-35 (Liv) became meaningful to me at that time. 'If any of you wants to be My follower, ...you must put aside your own pleasures and shoulder your cross, and follow Me closely. If you insist on saving your life, you will lose it. Only those who throw away their lives for My sake and for the sake of the Good News will ever know what it means to really live.' I had no idea what was ahead. Going was a step of obedience in following the Lord. A friend said to me, 'He knows, He loves, He cares. Nothing this truth can dim. He gives His very best to those who leave the choice with Him.'

"We loved Nigeria from the very beginning. There were adjustments and things we had to learn to get along without, but God richly replaced anything we gave. I remember the story of David Livingston when he spoke to a group of scholars in England, and they talked about his sacrifice. He had an arm that had been chewed by a lion, and the signs of suffering for the Lord were very evident in his body. He said, 'I could never use the word sacrifice for the life God has given me in Africa.' I really feel that way, too.

"There was probably no time in the twenty-one years that we lived in Nigeria that we didn't have to trust God for at least two or three of the basic essentials of life. One time when it was Joy's birthday, we didn't have any baking powder to make her cake. She had friends coming over for her birthday, so we prayed that God would provide some baking powder. When I went to our mailbox, there was a tin of baking powder.

"Another time when the boys were small, we ran out of milk. That evening one of the Nigerians came with a gallon of milk he had driven a good half hour across town to bring.

"The doctor that Keith worked for had a compound of three houses, and we lived in one of those houses. It was next to a big mission compound where they had water towers to store water. Our compound didn't have any water towers, but we had two bathtubs, so I kept one bathtub for water storage. We could usually manage okay, but one time we went days without additional water. Finally, there was no water left. The missionaries next door had plenty of water. I said, 'Lord, I'm also a missionary. Why do we live here with nothing, and they have an abundance?' It was as if He answered me, 'What is that to you? Just follow Me. I can take care of what you need.' One day a water tanker pulled into our compound. We had just one small tank at ground level, and everybody used it. The water tanker filled up our water tank, and he came back every day until water was available again. It was as if the Lord was saying, 'Yes, you could live on a mission compound and not have to trust Me for water, but you have an opportunity that they totally missed of getting to watch Me provide the basic things that you need.'

"When David was three weeks old, we moved so Keith could work with the university. They were supposed to provide housing for us, but our house wasn't ready. For the next eighteen months we watched God provide twelve houses.

"One place was a semi-Nigerian compound. Some of the buildings were in front, then a big open space, and the other buildings were in back. We had to go through the rain to get to the bathroom, and it wasn't a very convenient situation. When I first saw it, I thought, 'Lord, do we really have to live here?' The thought came back very clearly, 'If I, the King of Glory choose to live here, who are you to say that you don't want to live here?' I quickly told the Lord that it was fine, and we saw God transform that place into His dwelling place.

"I have thought about that many times when I've been discontent with what God provides. If it's His gift to us, then who am I to complain?

"Our three children, Joy, Daniel, and David, basically spent all of their growing up years in Nigeria. It was the most wonderful place in all of the world for us to raise a family. Our ministry was a family ministry, and our home was the center of it. Today the fruit that we're seeing in the lives of our children is the result of people around the world who have been in our home and prayed for our children.

"After we moved back to the United States, I said, 'Lord, this is not for us!' Once again I would have opted for something easier. God, however, put us in a situation that was totally beyond what I felt we could handle and where we once again could see Him work.

"Isaiah 42:16 says, 'I will lead the blind by ways they have not known, along unfamiliar paths I will guide them; I will turn the darkness into light before them and make the rough places smooth. These are the things I will do; I will not forsake them.' The only qualification here is that I'm blind. If I'm blind, all I need is someone who can see, and I need that person to walk with me and to open up the way. That's what God said He will do.

"We're basically doing the very same thing here that we did in Africa. Once again our ministry is in the home, and the kids are very much a part of it. I feel that we are just as much on a mission field today as we ever were in Nigeria.

"Some favorite verses are Psalm 27:13 (Brk): 'What if I had not believed to see the Lord's goodness in the land of the living!' What if I hadn't believed God? What if I had chosen a different way? I think, 'Oh, Lord, what would I have missed if I hadn't chosen to deny myself and take up my cross and follow You?'

"Joe Bayley, who had two small children and an eighteen-year-old who died, said, 'Faith means something when it's exercised in darkness. Perhaps the only time it means something is when what we have faith about is totally absent.' He also said, 'God's primary purpose is not to shield us from suffering, but to make us like Jesus because we learn obedience through what we suffer.'

"It isn't the route that I would have chosen," continues Carol, "but I wouldn't trade one step of the way. Our desire is to know God and walk with Him in reality and to share Him with others. This is a vision and a deep conviction in our lives."

Give Me a Vision

Lord, I see the needs of others.
I see them everywhere.
People dying, in despair,
Where are the ones who care?

May I be aware of others
To see their hurts and needs,
To show them that you love them
By actions and by deeds.

Help me to share how You have come
To earth to set men free.
Free from bondage, sin and shame,
To live in victory.

And when I cannot see ahead,
By faith help me to know,
That You are there beside me
And that You love me so.

For every time I've needed You,
You've always been right there
With strength and help and miracles,
With tender love and care.

Yes, You've blessed me in so many ways.
You've blessed that I might share,
Share the love of Jesus Christ
With those still unaware.

Chapter 23

Don't Give Up!

My niece Jo and her three-year-old daughter Dawnya stayed with us for a few months while waiting to join her husband in Germany. One day Dawnya was looking for Uncle Shelly. After searching everywhere and not finding him, she came to me and said, "Aunt Mary, Uncle Shelly can't find me!"

When you feel like God "can't find you," that you're one in millions lost in the crowds, don't give up! You are not lost to God. Isaiah 43:1 says that He knows you by name! "Fear not, for I have redeemed you; I have summoned you by name; you are mine." God has promised He will never leave you. Deuteronomy 31:8 says, "The Lord Himself goes before you and will be with you; He will never leave you nor forsake you. Do not be afraid; do not be discouraged." You never need to fear being lost to God, for He always knows the way and is always with you.

When things look overwhelmingly big, when circumstances are whirling out of control, and when you want to throw up your hands in despair and quit, don't give up! God is there! God in His wisdom never gives us more than we can handle. He helps us take the first step, and the next, and the next, and so we walk in His strength, daily, hourly, and minute by minute. Sometimes we may feel like we're only taking baby steps, and sometimes we may even fall. But fellow believers and God Himself with multitudes of angels are there to encourage us on. "Get up! Keep going! You can make it!" Psalms 73:26 says, "My flesh and my heart may fail, but God is the strength of my heart and my portion forever."

We used to live very close to the Pacific Ocean in Oregon. One day we were at the beach and my dad, along with some of the other adults, was swimming. Suddenly, he was caught in a rip tide, an undercurrent that moves away from shore. He soon was carried further and further out into the ocean. In desperation he raised his hand toward heaven and said, "Oh, God, help me!" Instantly the tide changed, and he was carried back toward shore where others were able to rescue him. I remember the men laying him across a log, working to revive him and pumping water from his lungs. Outside of God, my dad would have drowned. It was truly a miracle! Five other people drowned that day. God in His mercy and power reversed the tide beneath him, and his life was saved. There is nothing too big for God! Even the waves and the wind obey Him.

As we have shared the personal true stories of several people in this book, the evidence of a God who cares and can use every circumstance in our lives to bring glory to Himself is evident. God is faithful! He is there and ready to help. Lamentations 3:22-23 says, "Because of the Lord's great love we are not consumed, for his compassions never fail. They are new every morning; great is your faithfulness."

Another great encouragement is the fact that God always keeps His promises! Joshua 23:14b tells us, "You know with all your heart and soul that not one of all the good promises the Lord your God gave you has failed. Every promise has been fulfilled; not one has failed."

At this very moment you may be facing some difficult trial or agonizing tragedy of your own. Remember, God's love will surround us as we walk through the valley, His power will take us safely to the other side, and His mercy will lead us safely home. When we finish this life and cross the line of eternity, Jesus will be there to greet us. What a joy it will be! What a hope to look forward to!

I Peter 1:4-6 (Liv) gives these encouraging words, "And God has reserved for His children the priceless gift of eternal life; it is kept in heaven for you, pure and undefiled, beyond the reach of change and decay. And God, in His mighty power, will make sure that you get there safely to receive it because you are trusting Him. It will be yours in that coming last day for all to see. So be truly glad! There is wonderful joy ahead, even though the going is rough for awhile down here."

I pray that you have been encouraged by those who have shared their stories with us. When you want to ask, "God, are you really there?", keep your eyes above and keep trusting in Him. He is there. Our Victory Day is coming. Don't give up!

We end with a great promise found in Revelations 21:4-7. "He will wipe every tear from their eyes. There will be no more death or mourning or crying or pain, for the old order of things has passed away. He who was seated on the throne said, 'I am making everything new!' Then he said, 'Write this down, for these words are trustworthy and true.' He said to me: 'It is done. I am the Alpha and the Omega, the Beginning and the End. To him who is thirsty I will give to drink without cost from the spring of the water of life. He who overcomes will inherit all this, and I will be his God and he will be my son."

"Now may the Lord of peace Himself continually grant you peace in every circumstance. The Lord be with you all!" 2 Thessalonians 3:16 (NASU)

Don't Give Up!

Don't give up when circumstances
Are more than you can bear.
When a day seems like forever,
And you're in deep despair.

For John recorded in God's Word,
A record that is true.
A day is soon approaching
When all will be made new.

He saw the New Jerusalem,
One made with precious stone,
Where walls of jasper, streets of gold,
And jewels round it shone.

In transparent crystal prisms
The colors shone so bright,
In reds and yellows, greens and blues
Of rainbow colored light.

And yet in all this glorious scene,
The jewels not mentioned are
The ones that Christ will make His own,
The jewels most dear by far.

For when we cross the other shore
And heaven's home we share,
He says that we will be His jewels
When we are gathered there.

Here God will live among all men
And wipe away their tears,
No more crying, death, or sorrow,
And no more pain or fears.

To the thirsty He'll give water
Abundantly and free
From springs that never will run dry,
That flow eternally.

Yes, life is but a moment,
And though there's sorrow here,
A wondrous day is coming
When Jesus will appear.

Just lift your eyes and look above,
For victory's on its way!
Christ will come back and there will be
The final triumph day!